CODAR 830

RETIREMENT COUNSELING

SERIES IN DEATH EDUCATION, AGING, AND HEALTH CARE

HANNELORE WASS, CONSULTING EDITOR

ADVISORY BOARD

Herman Feifel, Ph.D.
Jeanne Quint Benoliel, R.N., Ph.D.
Balfour Mount, M.D.

Benoliel—*Death Education for the Health Professional*
Corless, Pittman-Lindeman—*AIDS: Principles, Practices, and Politics, Abridged Edition*
Corless, Pittman-Lindeman—*AIDS: Principles, Practices, and Politics, Reference Edition*
Curran—*Adolescent Suicidal Behavior*
Davidson—*The Hospice: Development and Administration, Second Edition*
Degner, Beaton—*Life–Death Decisions in Health Care*
Doty—*Communication and Assertion Skills for Older Persons*
Epting, Neimeyer—*Personal Meanings of Death: Applications of Personal Construct Theory to Clinical Practice*
Haber—*Health Care for an Aging Society: Cost-Conscious Community Care and Self-Care Approaches*
Lund—*Older Bereaved Spouses: Research with Practical Applications*
Prunkl, Berry—*Death Week: Exploring the Dying Process*
Riker, Myers—*Retirement Counseling: A Practical Guide for Action*
Sherron, Lumsden—*Introduction to Educational Gerontology, Third Edition*
Stillion—*Death and the Sexes: An Examination of Differential Longevity, Attitudes, Behaviors, and Coping Skills*
Stillion, McDowell, May—*Suicide across the Life Span—Premature Exits*
Turnbull—*Terminal Care*
Vachon—*Occupational Stress in the Care of the Critically Ill, the Dying, and the Bereaved*
Wass, Berardo, Neimeyer—*Dying: Facing the Facts, Second Edition*
Wass, Corr—*Childhood and Death*
Wass, Corr—*Helping Children Cope with Death: Guidelines and Resources, Second Edition*
Wass, Corr, Pacholski, Forfar—*Death Education II: An Annotated Resource Guide*
Wass, Corr, Pacholski, Sanders—*Death Education: An Annotated Resource Guide*
Weenolsen—*Transcendence of Loss over the Life Span*

IN PREPARATION

Bard—*Medical Ethics in Practice*
Bertman—*The Language of Grief and the Art of Communication*
Brammer—*Coping with Life Transitions: The Challenge of Personal Change*
Leenars, Wenckstern—*Suicide Prevention in Schools*
Leng—*Psychological Care in Old Age*
Leviton—*Horrendous Death*
Lindeman, Corby, Downing, Sanborn—*Dementia Day-Care Handbook*
Lonetto—*Explaining Death and Dying*
Papadatos, Papadatou—*Children and Death*
Salloway, Matthiesen—*The Chosen Daughter: Women and Their Institutionalized Mothers*

HQ
1062
.R54
1990

RETIREMENT COUNSELING

A Practical Guide for Action

Harold C. Riker
Jane E. Myers

University of Florida

WITHDRAWN

●HEMISPHERE PUBLISHING CORPORATION
A member of the Taylor & Francis Group

New York   Washington   Philadelphia   London

HIEBERT LIBRARY 34643
Fresno Pacific College - M. B. Seminary
Fresno, Calif 93702

RETIREMENT COUNSELING: A Practical Guide for Action

Copyright © 1990 by Hemisphere Publishing Corporation. All rights reserved. Printed in the United States of America. Except as permitted under the United States Copyright Act of 1976, no part of this publication may be reproduced or distributed in any form or by any means, or stored in a data base or retrieval system, without the prior written permission of the publisher.

1 2 3 4 5 6 7 8 9 0   B R B R   8 9 8 7 6 5 4 3 2 1 0 9

This book was set in Times Roman by Hemisphere Publishing Corporation. The editors were Susan E. Zinninger and Deborah Klenotic; the production supervisor was Peggy M. Rote; and the typesetters were Laurie Agee and Linda Andros.
Cover design by Debra Eubanks Riffe.
Braun-Brumfield, Inc. was printer and binder.

Library of Congress Cataloging in Publication Data

Riker, Harold C.
    Retirement counseling.

    Includes bibliographies and index.
    1. Retirement—United States.   2. Retirees—Counseling
of—United States.   3. Life change events in old age—
United States.   I. Myers, Jane E.   II. Title.
HQ1062.R54 1990   306.3'8'0973   89-19745
ISBN 0-89116-628-9
ISSN 0275-3510

*To those older adults who want to continue growing
and living more effectively and
to those counselors who want to help them do so.*

Contents

Preface

This handbook presents retirement as a time for a new beginning in one's life. In the past, this period of life has been viewed generally as a signal for separation from full-time employment, for withdrawal, for being taken care of through pensions and government subsidies, and for a variety of personal losses.

In the future, it is hoped, this life period will become better understood as a time for personal renewal, offering possibilities for major positive changes in lifestyle and providing new opportunities for continued personal growth.

Signs of impending changes in the commonly held views of retirement may be found in some of the current trends relating to older persons. First, life expectancy has shown remarkable growth in the 20th century to an average of 71.2 years for men and 78.2 years for women as of 1985, with more and more people living past 100 years of age. Men who reach 65 years of age can expect to live 14.8 more years, to about 80; in the case of women, they can expect to live 18.6 more years, to about age 84. On this basis, older persons today can look forward to more years for living.

Second, individuals are retiring from full-time employment at earlier ages. The average age for retirement has dropped from age 65 to age 62, with sizable numbers retiring at earlier ages. With earlier retirement and longer life expectancies, it will be important to their life satisfaction for older adults to find new interests and additional activities for the longer retirement period.

Third, more older adults are already participating in physical exercise programs, engaging in a variety of volunteer activities, travelling widely, and taking part-time jobs. These persons are demonstrating some of the possibilities for an active retirement.

But additional social and economic problems could be ahead for our country as more and more persons live longer and healthier lives and greater numbers of our citizens remain active in the third major period of life, after education and work, called *retirement*.

For purposes of illustration, let us assume that most individuals work full time from about age 30 to age 60, retire, and increasingly live reasonably active lives from age 60 to age 90. The time is soon approaching when individuals will live in their retirement period approximately the same number of years that they worked full time.

Particular social and economic questions will then arise: What kinds of lifestyles will these retirees live? How will they be financially supported?

As a society, we have generally taken the medical approach to aging and older persons. When persons become sick, we attempt to cure them, or at least to make them more comfortable. The federal and state programs of Medicare and Medicaid demonstrate the tremendous amount of the financial commitment to this medical approach. However, this approach may become difficult to follow as the numbers of older persons increase and more funds are required to care for them.

An alternative to the medical approach to aging is the wellness approach, which seeks to prevent sickness and help older persons to remain well and functioning as independently as possible. It would appear that the direction for the future is not to be found in building more nursing homes, but in developing more wellness programs that encourage and facilitate regular physical examinations for older persons, physical exercise and nutrition programs, and stress-control instructions on a communitywide basis. Also important is the development of positive views toward living by older persons themselves.

The older persons in this country have much to offer, in terms of their diverse experience and abilities, in many fields. Rather than being viewed as liabilities to our society, older persons should be seen as assets. However, they need to feel that they are assets and realize that they have important contributions to make to their communities, states, and nation.

This handbook is focused also on mental health counselors, as professionals especially qualified to assist older persons in their discovery of new lifestyles. Such counselors can help older persons to better understand themselves as capable human beings and active and contributing members of their communities. Counselors can encourage older persons to see the retirement period of their lives as a time to develop abilities that may have been latent and possibly even discouraged.

Through their actions, counselors can encourage older persons to recognize that they have continuing potentials to be discovered and used. In this process of self-discovery they can strengthen their own fellings of self-worth and understand that they can indeed add to the well-being of this country of which they are an integral part. By their own actions, they must help in overcoming the prejudices against aging and older persons that persist in this nation.

There are indications that both the public and private sectors of our society are seeing older persons in a new light and with renewed appreciation. For example, some state governments are developing programs that encourage older persons to maintain independent living in their own homes. In the private sector, various companies are making it possible for older employees to remain on their jobs; others are hiring older workers. Such activities are to be encouraged by all those who share with us the dual viewpoint that, first, older persons should be encouraged to follow additional avenues of interest and activity, and, second, retirement is a new frontier to be explored and developed because of its own intrinsic value as the third major period of the human life span.

This handbook is intended for two groups: those planning to retire or already retired and professional counselors who plan to assist older persons in their transitions to retirement.

For the first group, this handbook can help to clarify their views about their own retirement, plan for their daily living in retirement, gain a better understanding of important issues in their retirement, and take appropriate action regarding those issues. For the second group, this handbook can help to enlarge their understanding of aging as a growth process, with individuals having continuing potentials as they grow older; and it can also expand their knowledge about the issues retirees face and the opportunities to be found in retirement.

Eleven chapters are presented, each of which includes sections on implications for counselors and suggested group activities. These activities can be used by counselors in classes for graduate students or modified only slightly for groups of older persons who are considering retirement issues and opportunities. At the beginning of each chapter is a brief overview of topics included in the chapter.

Harold C. Riker
Jane E. Myers

Chapter One

Retirement Is a Modern Myth

INTRODUCTION

Retirement is much misunderstood. For some, it is a welcome release from work; for others, it is the end of an active, useful life. It can mean fishing, golfing, or playing, without time deadlines and time schedules; it can also mean decline in capabilities and capacities, with fewer associations and reduced involvements.

For some, retirement is an opportunity to create new ways of living, try out activities they have long wanted to try, build new approaches to daily living, find out who they are, and express feelings and ideas about themselves more completely. For them, retirement is a filling out of life in satisfying though sometimes unexpected ways. People mold their own lives as they grow and develop. The retirement years are no exception.

Two distinct and very different images of retired people exist in the United States today. One image is the hale and hearty older person 65 years of age or more, appearing to be in good physical condition, active in outdoor activities, participating in community organizations, and enjoying life. The second image is an infirm and sickly older person, 85 years of age or more, being cared for around the clock, in a wheelchair or bed, not very happy with life in general, perhaps living in a nursing home.

In short, health and activity are sometimes linked with age, though usually sickness, infirmity, inactivity, isolation, and unhappiness are more commonly visualized. To illustrate, a 70-year-old man, upon reaching his 70th birthday, said, "Well, I'll have to give up my exercise program and my social activities and be old." Everyone who grows older, and everyone does, has a choice: to pursue an active lifestyle or to sit back and be "old."

In this chapter, common stereotypes about aging are described, along with their inconsistencies with reality. Some of the factors that contribute to these stereotypes include the established chronological age for retirement, reactions to retirement, and definitions of retirement. Historical changes in the meaning of retirement are reviewed. Implications of these changes for counselors are suggested and group activities are listed that are intended to help participants visualize some of the opportunities in retirement.

RETIREMENT MYTHS

Attitudes that individuals have toward their retirement grow out of the attitudes of the society of which they are a part. In general, American society has viewed retirement as the arrival of old age, a condition generally regarded as undesirable. Losses are seen as inevitable: loss of job, loss of income, and, most of all, loss of identity. Retirement is believed to be followed by physical deterioration accompanied by sickness, and sickness by helplessness. Mental health is assumed to decline, with depression as a frequent occurrence. Feelings of worthlessness are viewed as inevitable. The myths are so powerful that many people are convinced that they can do nothing but accept them. Often, their friends and relatives reinforce the myths, in indirect but influential ways, such as alluding to negative expectations for the retirement years.

Stereotypes About Aging

Retirement myths are supported and reinforced by various stereotypes of aging. The total impact of these stereotypes can be understood better when they are reviewed together. The first is the definition of being old on the basis of chronological years. Being 65 or 70 years of age is commonly seen as being old. However, chronological years are imprecise indicators of age. Some people are young at 80 years of age, others are old at 40 years. According to Butler, there are great differences in the rates of physiological, chronological, psychological, and social aging, both within the same person, and from one person to another (1).

A second stereotype is that older persons are unproductive and therefore useless. For many years, mandatory retirement policies supported this stereotype. However, barring disease and social adversity, many older persons are productive and actively involved in a variety of enterprises. The fact is that older workers can be as effective as younger workers, except perhaps in jobs requiring prolonged physical stamina and rapid response behaviors.

A third stereotype is that older persons prefer to withdraw from social activity and to live alone or perhaps with a few peers. The emphasis is on less interaction with others and on living with memories of the past. This stereotype describes the theory of disengagement and explains the behavior of some older persons, but not all. Many are actively involved in the lives of their communities, as illustrated by their participation in federal programs such as Senior Companions, Foster Grandparents, and Retired Senior Volunteers. Other older adults are active in national, regional, and local organizations of the American Association of Retired Persons, which reports a combined membership of some 30 million persons.

A fourth stereotype is that older persons are inflexible, insistent on following set patterns of behavior, and unwilling to consider change. Older persons may prefer the familiar and fear change which involves the unknown. But so do many persons regardless of age. In fact, the capacity to change and adapt seems to be related more to lifelong behavior patterns than to age. Yet, the stereotype of inflexibility is associated with older adults (2).

"You can't teach an old dog new tricks" is a common expression of the stereotype that older persons experience a declining ability to learn. Related to this stereotype is the popular belief that intelligence decreases with age. In actuality, healthy older persons can continue to increase their ability to organize their thinking and successfully complete a college degree program. Recent research has led to a distinction between *fluid* and *crystallized* intelligence. Fluid intelligence, the ability to learn new things, decreases slightly with age. Crystallized intelligence, or stored funds of knowledge, continues to increase, while the overall pattern is one of no change or only slight change in intelligence with age. The decrease in fluid intelligence actually reflects a decrease in response speed. Some research suggests that older persons can be helped to improve their response speed on intelligence tests (3); hence, their scores may be expected to improve. Yet, the popular opinion is that older persons' ability to learn continues to decline.

Another stereotype is that older persons are senile, meaning that they are forgetful, confused, or unable to keep focused on one topic for any period of time. Undiagnosed and largely reversible problems, such as anxiety, grief, depression, overuse of drugs, or malnutrition, may produce the behaviors described as senile. However, permanent brain damage, correctly identified as senility, is irreversible. The point is that much of the behavior called senility can be successfully treated.

Yet another commonly held stereotype is that older persons have a declining capacity for sexual activity. This stereotype has two components. The first is the frequently held belief that sexual relationships for older persons are improper. The second is the impression that older persons lose with age their physiological capacities for intercourse. The evidence is that healthy older persons who have maintained reasonable continuity in their sex lives continue to enjoy sexual relationships throughout most of the life span (4).

Another stereotype is that serenity is the reward of those who grow older. The impression conveyed by this stereotype is that the problems of active life are over, that older persons accept whatever befalls them. In actuality, older persons often face as many stressful conditions as other age groups, or even more. Although growing older is unlikely to eliminate stress, the fact of survival over a long period of time does seem to equip older persons to deal adequately with various stresses when they arise.

The total impact of these and other false beliefs about aging cannot be calculated. However, their effect on persons planning to retire can be described as negative and as painting the picture of a dismal, decaying future which hardly seems worth the effort. The social prejudice thus confronting older Americans can discourage efforts toward continued growth and continued interest in developing new capabilities. Yet, when older persons understand the stereotypes about aging as expressions of prejudice they can look ahead with anticipation to the opportunities of their future. They will also find it helpful to gain more factual information about the aging process and about the life changes to which they should react.

There are several issues involving retirement which contribute to some of the stereotypes already mentioned. These include (a) the age for retirement, (b) the definition of retirement, and (c) reactions to retirement. These issues are discussed below, followed by a historical review of changes in the meaning of retirement.

The Time for Retirement

First, when is retirement? Age 65 has been the commonly accepted age for retirement. In 1932, Social Security legislation specified 65 as the age at which citizens would be eligible for retirement benefits.

However, the trend is toward earlier retirement. The age at which more people retire at present is 62, and the average is dropping. For example, active duty military personnel can retire after 20 years of service, as early as ages 38–40. Many blue-collar workers now retire in their middle and late 50s. Organizations such as labor unions, the federal Civil Service, and some corporations have even encouraged earlier retirement.

In the fall of 1986, federal legislation abolished the retirement age of 70. Some states have canceled any age limitations on employment. In terms of human rights, legislation has been in the direction of enabling all citizens to work as long as they have the skill and will to work.

In spite of opportunities to retire at older ages, more people are retiring at younger ages. The point is that the age of retirement varies widely and may vary even more in the future. Retirees no longer represent a particular age group, if they ever did; their ages range upward from 40.

Definition of Retirement

Some definitions of retirement are detailed and long, because definers try to be inclusive. However, all definitions seem to include two major features: (a) Retired persons are employed less than full time, and (b) their income is derived, in part at least, from retirement pensions.

Retirement is part of an occupational role. It is an event, a process, or a social role (5). In terms of an event and an occupational process, retirement in U.S. society is likely to emphasize finality. As a social role, however, it can have an ongoing quality, bringing new opportunities and new responsibilities. This role usually involves new kinds of relationships with family, former job associates, neighbors, and friends. It also is likely to bring with it new friends and new associates.

Since decision making in the past may have been handled by one's job supervisor, new freedom of action in retirement will call for decisions on one's own and more self-reliance. Since financial resources can be expected to drop for most persons, revisions in style of living may be in order. Since self-identity is often derived from one's job, the retiree may wonder, "Who am I? What do I want to be now and in the future?" Out of the answers to these questions a revised identity can develop.

Retirement may represent a new beginning in the retiree's life, comparable in some ways to the younger person's leaving home for a first job. There are differences. The older person has the advantages of varied past experiences upon which to draw for guidance; the younger person does not. The younger person views the future as infinite; the older person knows that it is not.

Reactions to Retirement

Emotional reactions to retirement range widely, from eager anticipation to sullen anger. In general, there tends to be a significant difference in reaction between blue-collar and white-collar workers, or on the basis of the amount of independent responsibility individuals have had on the job. Given an adequate amount of income on which to live comfortably, blue-collar workers tend to favor retirement, whereas white-collar workers do not (6).

What are major factors influencing attitudes toward retirement? First, perhaps, is finances (7). However, past surveys have indicated that the majority of retirees have reported that their income was sufficient for their needs (8). Second is the physiological aging process, including the results of disease. There is often a gradual slowing down in reaction time, which may produce feelings of inadequacy. Intellectual processes also seem to change with age; some persons experience a decline in functioning, some do not. For most persons, the ability to learn effectively remains.

The third factor is psychological state, which is closely interrelated with biological condition. In their later years, most persons experience a life review process that can be both positive and negative (9). To deal with feelings of guilt and their causes can bring about resolutions of unhappy memories and lead to feelings of relief and satisfaction. To relive past failures without recognizing that they are no longer important can rekindle and reinforce negative feelings.

Decline in physical strength and changes in physical appearance can be devastating to both men and women. In the case of men who have associated strength with masculinity, the experiencing of physical limitations in retirement can undermine the sense of personal identity as a male. In the case of women who have valued physical beauty and youthful appearance, changes occurring with age can lead to doubts of personal worth. To be sought by both men and women in retirement is a reassessment of personal values, a better understanding of the aging process, and the creation of new lifestyles.

Persons who are retiring or have retired are to be encouraged to develop a new social status for themselves through greater attention to personal growth, more meaningful relationships with others, more satisfying uses of leisure activities, and more appreciation of the world around them, both physical and social.

CHANGES IN THE MEANING OF RETIREMENT

When the United States was an agrarian society, most individuals lived and worked on the farm. When they were no longer able to work, they continued to live with family members on the farm. Since life expectancy in 1900 was 44 years for men and 49 for women (10), retirement was not a serious concern. With the development of an industrial economy in the latter part of the 1800s, pensions and mandatory retirement came into being. Pensions were used as incentives for experienced workers to remain at their jobs. The longer they worked, the greater would be their retirement income. Mandating retirement served as a way for management to counteract seniority rules fostered by labor unions and to require infirm workers to leave their jobs. Aging was not the primary consideration (11).

During the 20th century, developments in technology and the resulting speed-up in work routine led to the preferred employment of younger men. The Depression of the 1930s created terrible conditions of poverty in the United States (and elsewhere), particularly for older persons.

Financial Aid for Older Persons

In 1935, the U.S. Congress adopted the Social Security Act, which was intended to provide for old-age security, especially for the older poor. This legislation designated age 65 as the eligible age for retirement and created an insurance system to guarantee pensions for retired and disabled workers and for their survivors. This act also stipulated that recipients not be employed.

From 1945 to 1955, labor unions began to include pensions in their negotiations with management, and companies were permitted to count contributions to pension plans as business deductions. In this period, private pension plans were expanded to cover more than 15 million workers (11).

The federal government continued its support of older citizens through the Older Americans Act, passed first in 1965, with subsequent revisions in the 1970s (12). The stated objectives for older persons included an adequate income in retirement; the best possible physical and mental health available through science; suitable housing; full restoration care through community-based, long-term care services; opportunity for employment without discrimination because of age; retirement in health, honor, and dignity; pursuit of civic, cultural, educational, and recreational activities; benefits from research designed to sustain and improve health and happiness; and freedom to plan and manage their lives and participate in the planning and operation of services designed for their benefit.

Services included in this act were home delivery of nutritious meals and senior recreational centers, homemakers assistance and home improvement, and friendly visitors and transportation. Provision of information and referral, as well as legal services, were included. A national network of area agencies on aging was created to organize and supervise these various services.

Also in 1965, Medicare was established to remove financial obstacles to medical care for disabled adults and older people. Its two parts are hospital insurance and medical insurance. Payroll deductions and special premiums were intended to pay for this federal health insurance program.

Medicaid, also part of the Social Security system, but financed on a matching basis with state funds, was developed to provide certain health services for the older poor who receive Supplementary Security Income and other individuals who receive federally aided public assistance. This program supports care on a long-term maintenance basis or to prevent deterioration. The various states administer this program.

Additional Federal Initiatives

Additional federal legislation aimed at improving the quality of life for older persons included the Age Discrimination in Employment Act (1967) and the Employees Retirement Income Security Act (1974) intended to make certain that private pension plans produced or carried through on promises made for income after retirement.

From 1935 to 1980, the federal government developed and implemented programs designed to keep older people above the poverty level, to furnish medical care in order to raise the level of physical health, and to provide for higher levels of quality of life in retirement. Undoubtedly, this federal effort had been encouraged by several national organizations of older persons, including the American Association of Retired Persons (AARP), the National Council on the Aging, and the National Council of Senior Citizens. The AARP currently claims more than 30 million members who make this organization a potent political advocacy group.

Both the federal initiatives, which have fostered training and research in the field of aging, and the growth of organizations, which have focused public attention on the well-being of older persons in the separate states and nationally, have served to bring new meanings to the term retirement. Through the various news media, the general public is gaining a new image of retired persons, as healthy, active, and involved in a wide range of community enterprises. Many older persons have been relieved in some measure of the pressures of economic and health problems; many can and do enjoy the company of peers in informal settings; some assist the young or the sick through a variety of volunteer services; and some maintain part-time employment.

In the recent past, retired older persons were visualized as patients in nursing homes, yet the facts are that no more than 5% are institutionalized at any one time. Another 15% receive some assistance to remain living independently in the community or in group living facilities such as Adult Congregate Living Facilities. The remaining people who are 65 years of age or older live relatively independent, satisfied lives. In fact, the great majority of older persons are in good physical and mental health. They are self-sufficient and lead rewarding lives (13).

State Initiatives

The U.S. Congress has become increasingly aware of the problems of the rapidly growing older population and has sought solutions to many of them. Some state governments are attempting to move beyond the solving of older people's problems to the *prevention* of their problems. For example, in 1986 the Florida Committee on Aging addressed the goals of physical and economic self-sufficiency for Florida's older citizens (13). Recommendations for health programs included the following:

1 Provide annual physical examinations based on an ability-to-pay system in county public health units, private clinics, or physicians' offices.

2 Expand county public health unit capacity to assess wellness needs and develop wellness projects.

3 Establish health promotion, prevention, and wellness pilot projects at senior centers within geographical areas of the state.

4 Develop a Medicaid-funded dental program.

5 Support research on ways to detect and prevent or reduce chronic diseases in the early years.

6 Organize specialized prevention and early intervention teams in community mental health programs to treat mental health problems of older people.

Recommendations for economic programs included the following:

1 Eliminate current postretirement employment restrictions in the state retirement system.

2 Expand hiring of older persons in state agencies, particularly as service providers to older clients and to children.

3 Develop a statewide media campaign to increase employer and older worker awareness of skills available among older workers.

4 Challenge private and public employers to recruit, train, and hire older workers.

Clearly, the goals of the Florida Committee on Aging could be adapted to the particular conditions of the remaining 49 states. If such goals were implemented on a nationwide basis, the negative impact of retirement would be drastically altered for millions of older persons.

Summary

The concept of retirement is little more than 100 years old. It began as a management method to counteract the labor unions' seniority rules that kept on the payroll older workers unable to perform. It was maintained to make room for younger workers. It was promoted as an opportunity for workers to enjoy the results of their labor. For the most part, however, retirement has been seen as a loss of work, income, and friends.

More recently, as people live longer, in better health, and with more financial resources to provide for a more comfortable standard of living, retirement is being viewed more favorably. It is our contention that when retirement becomes a means for individuals to create new lifestyles for better living for themselves, retirement will become an integral part of life planning.

IMPLICATIONS FOR COUNSELORS

Counselors have many opportunities to assist individuals of all ages with their life planning. As they work with those who are approaching midlife or later life, counselors and those individuals concerned should keep in mind the wide range of issues affecting planning for the later years. Many of these are discussed in detail in the remaining chapters of this book. A few that relate most closely to this chapter are listed below. Counselors need to be aware of these issues and their implications in order to be helpful to persons as they age.

Retirement is a modern myth, largely focused on the work experiences of the 20th century and largely negative in connotation. It is a consequence of the occupational role and process. It is associated with loss of job, loss of income, and loss of friends and associates. Frequently, retirement is equated with sickness and death. As a result, individuals recognizing retirement as a foreseeable future event are likely to have negative emotional reactions.

However, some changes in the value system of our society seem to be occurring, particularly with reference to work. In earlier years, work was seen as an end in itself—a part of the Protestant work ethic. At the present time, work is largely regarded as a means to an end, that end being material possessions, leisure time activities, and the enjoyment of living.

With this perception of work, retirement becomes a time to take pleasure in the results of the individual's work effort. Retirement becomes a time of fulfillment.

In American society, a strong current of concern has developed for the well-being of deprived groups of people. In the Great Depression, it was the poor, especially the elderly poor. In the 1960s, it was the Black minority. In the 1960s and 1970s, it was older people and women. In the 1980s, disadvantaged and abused children as well as adults and the Hispanic minority have been targeted.

Out of this current of concern have come active roles for federal and state governments to assist older people with minimum income through Social Security; those with minimum health care through Medicare, Medicaid, and other special community programs; those with minimum social activities through senior centers and various community programs.

An emerging approach to the well-being of older people in retirement is the development of cooperative efforts on the part of public and private sectors of society toward finding and building solutions to problems. An important element of this partnership is the older persons themselves. They, too, have an important stake in their own well-being.

In fact, persons anticipating or experiencing retirement should be in charge of their own life planning whenever possible and should take responsibility not only for setting personal goals in retirement but also for developing strategies for reaching these goals. To illustrate, older persons can assume more personal responsibility for their own health plans, calling upon their physicians for specialized, technical advice.

Preparing for retirement should be understood to be as significant to the individual as preparing for entry into the world of work.

GROUP ACTIVITIES

I Goals in Retirement

Divide the participants into groups of about 7–10 persons each. Then ask them to assume that they are planning to retire and do the following:

1 Write down on a sheet of paper three activities they had wanted to accomplish all their lives, but had never found the opportunity to accomplish.

2 Place the three activities in priority order of importance for the person to accomplish.

3 Outline on the same sheet of paper a strategy for accomplishing the first priority activity in retirement.

Ask group members to share their priority activity and their strategy for accomplishment in small groups. Discuss reactions in the full group at the end of the session.

II Clarifying Values in Retirement

Divide participants into groups of approximately 7–10 persons each. Ask participants to do the following:

1 List on a sheet of paper five major values that have governed their actions in their work career.

2 Place these values in order of priority.

3 When they review their work career, have participants note whether these values have changed and if the priority has changed during their careers to date.

4 Then list on the same sheet of paper, five major values that they anticipate will govern their actions in retirement.

5 Place these values in priority order.

Ask group members to share their priority values for their career, and for their retirement. Discuss their reactions in the full group following the small group session.

REFERENCES

1 Butler, R. N. (1975). *Why survive? Being old in America.* New York: Harper and Row.

2 Hendricks, J. & Hendricks, C. D. (1981). *Aging in Mass Society. Myths and Realities,* Cambridge, MD: Winthrop.

3 Boltes, P., & Schale, K. (1974, March). The myth of the twilight years. *Psychology Today, 40,* 35–38.

4 Saxon, S. V., & Etter, M. J. (1983). *Physical change and aging: A guide for the helping profession.* New York: Tinesurs Press.

5 Atchley, R. (1977). *The social forces in later life: An introduction to social gerontology.* Belmont, CA: Wadsworth.

6 Sheppard, H. C. (1976). Work and Retirement. In R. H. Binstock & E. Shanas (Eds.), *Handbook of Aging and the Social Sciences* (pp. 286–309). New York: Van Nostrand Reinltold.

7 Barfield, R. E., & Morgan, J. N. (1978). Trends in satisfaction with retirement. *The Gerontologist, 18*(1), 19–23.

8 Harris, L., & Associates. (1975). *The myth and reality of aging in America.* Washington, DC: National Council on the Aging.

9 Butler, R. N. (1963). The life review: An interpretation of reminiscence in the aged. *Psychiatry, 26,* 65–76.

10 U. S. Senate Special Committee on Aging. (1985-1986). *Aging America.* Washington, DC: Author.

11 Atchley, R. (1985). *Social forces and aging.* Belmont, CA: Wadsworth.

12 Oberle, J. (1981). The aging network. In J. E. Myers, P. Finnerty-Fried, & C. Graves (Eds.), *Counseling older persons* (Vol. 1, pp. 11–18). Alexandria, VA: American Association for Counseling and Development.

13 Florida Committee on Aging. (1986). *Pathways to the future.* Tallahassee, FL: Author.

Chapter Two

Living Is a Continuing Process

Life does not stop with retirement; life continues. Living is a series of actions, a sequence of changes; it is a process during which individuals change many, many times. Change may be almost imperceptible at any given point in the life span. Change may also be described as "growth" especially during the first part of life, from babyhood through the early 30s. Visual physical change or growth during life's middle part from the early 30s through the early 60s, may be less obvious; at this time of life behaviors may represent the focus of change.

During the third part of life after the fifth or sixth decade, change, either visual or behavioral, is most often seen as "decline." The difference between change described as "growth" and change described as "decline" is often to be found in the attitude and frame of reference of the beholder.

Many persons in U.S. society have been conditioned to place high values on the physical and the material. Growth in these terms is readily understood, and so is decline. In terms of the mental and the spiritual, however, growth is more likely to be felt than seen, primarily through interpersonal relationships. Perhaps the root of the problem of negative attitudes toward aging and older people is the common failure to recognize their continued growth potential, partly because it cannot be easily seen or measured.

All persons have the potential to grow. For some, that potential may be limited; for others, it may be almost unlimited. The potentials of younger persons lie in the direction of selecting an area of work, starting a family, developing financial independence, and establishing a position in the community.

The potentials for older persons build on those developed in earlier years and extend in other directions: maintaining a capacity for physical and mental health, strengthening friendships and relationships with others, and building a storehouse of wisdom from past and present experiences and being willing to share it with others.

Additional important potentials for older persons are for enlarging their capacity for caring, loving, and discovering areas for creative activity. Examples in the contemporary United States include Bob Hope and George Burns in the field of entertainment, Claude Pepper in the field of politics, and Maggie Kuhn in the field of elder rights activism, all of whom are in their 80s or 90s.

The purpose of this chapter is to indicate that the human life span is a continuing sequence of events from birth through death and the later period of life is an integral and important part of the totality of experiences. (Chapter 4 concentrates on factors involved in planning to make the most of one's total life span.) Living is discussed as a developmental process in which persons can progress through a connected series of life stages. Five major life arenas are reviewed to show the diversity, yet relatedness, of human activities. The impact of change is stressed. Implications for counselors are listed and group activities suggested as means for deepening their understanding of the life process.

Two factors are of considerable importance in older persons' development of their potential in later life. The first is their attitudes and the second is their environment.

ATTITUDES

Attitudes are predispositions to respond to objects, persons, or situations in a particular way. Of special concern in the case of older persons are attitudes toward aging, work, leisure, significant others, and self.

Many persons have been conditioned by our society to equate getting older with sickness, poor health, and isolation. Older persons themselves have sometimes reflected this negative view by attempting to maintain youthful self-images, refusing to reveal their actual ages, and creating some inconsistencies between their view of themselves and their views of people around them. Some 80-year-olds often refer negatively to "those old people." There is a tendency for people to fear aging, to feel that the later part of life has no promise, and to see death looming threateningly over older persons, limiting any initiatives for action.

Attitudes toward work influence the behavior of people in later life. For many years in the United States, work was regarded as an end in itself. Self-identity was long defined in terms of what a person did for a living. However, work in and of itself does not seem to be as important to today's workers. Many have jobs that they describe as boring or unfulfilling. Blue-collar workers tend to look forward to retirement more than professional people, who tend to find their work rewarding (1). Greater automation in the factory and the office reduces workers' feelings of personal involvement with the product of their work. The amount of income in retirement appears to be a key element in workers' attitudes toward retirement. If they have sufficient income, they look forward to their time for retiring (2).

Attitudes toward leisure also have changed. Earlier in the 20th century, workers often saw leisure as the opposite of work and therefore of no value. In more recent years, leisure has become release time from work, when individuals can enjoy activities that vary along a continuum from relaxation and diversion through personal development and creativity for its own sake. Today's younger persons often fill their evenings and weekends with a variety of activities, from sports and recreation to community service projects. Focused on work, older persons sometimes fear that they will have too much free time in retirement. Several factors affect attitudes toward leisure in retirement. One is adequate income that permits older persons to participate in leisure activities (3). A second is a leisure ethic that gives legitimacy to such activities. A third factor is education for leisure in which individuals learn positive points of view toward leisure and the necessary skills to participate in appropriate activities (4). Regrettably, those who have not been educated in leisure often do not devote much time to these activities, particularly older people (5). It is apparent that education for leisure should begin early, even in childhood. A fourth factor for most people in many activities is often a leisure partner.

The attitudes of older persons are also influenced by the attitudes of significant others, such as family members and friends (6). For example, if fellow workers are strongly opposed to retirement, the reaction of other older workers is also likely to be negative. Negative attitudes toward aging on the part of family members are frequently contagious. On the other hand, retirement is more readily accepted when endorsed by family and friends.

Most important are the attitudes of older persons toward themselves. When older persons regard themselves as worthy, feel reasonably satisfied with their achievements, and continue to set goals for themselves, their attitudes toward themselves are likely to remain positive. But when the opposite situation exists, their attitudes often turn negative. The amazing situation about people, older or younger, is their apparent inertia in taking corrective action regarding themselves and their own negative attitudes. In contrast, they often will exert considerable effort to get some material possession functioning properly, such as their automobile.

The problem of attitudes, complex though it is, may be traced in part to a commonly held view of individual growth and development. This view of the human life span sees the first two stages, from birth through age 10, and the second, from age 11 through 20, as life stages of rapid and vigorous growth. The third stage, from 21 through 30, is a period of continued growth, but at a slower pace. The fourth, fifth, and sixth stages, ages 31 through 40, 41 through 50, and 51 through 60, respectively, are seen as life plateaus. Individuals in these three stages have attained maturity—so the thinking goes—and are reaping the rewards of their efforts. The seventh stage, from 61 to 70, is a time for deceleration, or slowing one's pace. The eighth and ninth stages, from ages 71 through 80 and 81 to 90, respectively, represent faster rates of decline (7).

Involved in this view of human development are values heavily weighted in favor of lifestyles experienced during the life segments of the 20s and 30s. According to a 1975 Harris Survey (8), 69% of the subjects interviewed nation-wide identified the teens, the 20s, and the 30s as "the best years of their lives." The age range of those interviewees was from 18 to 80 +. The 20s were chosen by those who saw this life period as one of limited responsibility and having fun. The life stage of the 30s was viewed as involving more experience and maturity, enjoyment of family, life, and "settling down."

The worst years of a person's life were believed to be the life periods of the 60s and 70s. Those seeing the teen years as difficult were primarily those in their 20s (8). Reasons for the negative views of the 60s and 70s included bad health, illness, financial problems, and physical limitations. Additional reasons were difficulty in finding jobs, retirement, loneliness, and little to look forward to. However, these expectations of the later years were expressed more by persons under 64 years of age and not by those over age 65 in the Harris study (8). An alternative view of development in later life is discussed later in this chapter.

ENVIRONMENT

Attitudes strongly influence the environments within which people live and work. Today's older persons have worked and matured within a society gener-ally focused on youth and prejudiced against old age. Today's older persons have observed the older cohorts of people ahead of them being moved aside to make room for younger persons. They have noted that many older persons take more passive roles in their families and communities. They have seen the ef-fects of declining physical vigor and ill health on older family members, former work associates, and friends.

In the home, today's adult children tend to reflect the negative societal attitudes and behaviors regarding older persons, and often reinforce these negative attitudes in their relationships with their own aging parents. For example, adult sons and daughters may offer to perform a simple task for their parents, thus expressing through their actions the view that the parents are no longer capable of carrying out that particular task for themselves. The motivation of the adult children may be to indicate a desire to help their parents. However, the implications are quite negative.

The adult child may fail to communicate with a parent or parents. The result can be that the parent feels isolated and no longer wanted. Such a problem might be resolved with greater understanding of changing roles by both younger and older family members, greater appreciation of the continuing potential of the older family members, and more open communication of personal feelings of affection, love, and respect by all concerned.

In the workplace, management frequently has demonstrated negative attitudes toward older workers. For a number of years, mandatory retirement policies were in force in this country. When older workers reached the age of 65 they understood that their employment would be terminated. According to the Harris Survey, mandatory retirement was generally not favored by many older workers (8). In more recent years, companies seeking to reduce operating costs have offered "early retirement" to their older workers. Financial incentives have tended to make job severance more palatable to these workers. At the same time, some feeling of discrimination against older workers has been conveyed.

In their communities, retired persons sometimes find themselves treated with an exaggerated respect by younger generations or belittled in more subtle ways. For example, a neighboring teenager may call out, "How are you going to spend your day, Grandpa? Now that you don't have a job?" While community organizations, such as senior centers, often provide excellent social activities for older citizens, these centers do have the effect of isolating older persons from the rest of the community. The communications media, newspapers, television, journals, and advertising have all emphasized the advantages of keeping young. Until the last few years, aging and older people have been portrayed in generally negative terms. In many facets of their living environments, older persons are reminded that they are indeed no longer part of the mainstream of family and community life.

The combined impact of attitudes and environments has done little to encourage older persons to keep on growing and developing their own potentials. In fact, the social attitudes and environments in this country suggest a failure of people in general to understand that there are important values in each stage of living. A new understanding of aging and growing older is desperately needed. Such an understanding can be gained through looking at human growth from a developmental perspective.

DEVELOPMENTAL VIEW OF LIVING

Several theorists have articulated a developmental view of human growth throughout the lifespan. Erikson (9) described life as a process of meeting and accomplishing eight major tasks, each one characterizing individual development during a particular life stage. Here is a listing of the tasks and the life stage identified with each:

Basic trust versus mistrust	Infancy (birth to 1 year)
Autonomy versus shame and doubt	Early childhood (1–3 years)
Initiative versus guilt	Childhood (3–6 years)
Industry versus inferiority	Middle childhood (6–12 years)
Identity versus role confusion	Adolescence (13–22 years)
Intimacy versus isolation	Young adulthood (22–30 years)
Generativity versus stagnation	Middle adulthood (30–50years)
Integrity versus despair	Late adulthood (50+ years)

Erikson believed (9) that from the early stages of life, individuals gain a sense of trust, feelings of self-control, and boundless energy if their experiences are positive. With the first school years, young people learn, it is hoped, to substitute work principles for play principles. During adolescence, they experience major physiological changes and begin to sense the role changes ahead of them. In these years their major concern is what others think of them. It is during this stage that one's ego identity is formed, from both the experiences of childhood and those of the present.

With the satisfactory formation of their ego identity, individuals are prepared for intimacy. According to Erikson, this stage is the ability to establish specific relationships with others and to commit oneself fully to those relationships regardless of the consequences. The next stage, generativity, was recognized by Erikson as a central one in human development. Concerned with learning and teaching, this stage is principally dedicated to assisting the next generation. The final stage, ego integrity, represents the fulfillment of the seven earlier stages. It is the acceptance of one's life as that life has developed; the persons with integrity are willing to defend their particular lifestyle against any opposition.

Erikson believed that human development occurs by critical stages and that these steps or stages are interdependent. He asserted that basic trust in the first stage of life can develop into strong faith in the last stage. At the same time, he made it clear that at each life stage, individuals can experience failure as well as success in their psychosocial development.

Havighurst (10) described living and growing as learning. To him, living involves many learning tasks, the successful accomplishment of which brings satisfaction and happiness. This theorist visualized six age periods: infancy and early childhood (0–5 years), middle childhood (6–12 years), adolescence (12–18 years), early adulthood (18–30 years), middle age (30–60 years), and late maturity (60+ years). For each age period, he listed 6–10 developmental tasks necessary for growth in our society.

These developmental tasks are physiological, psychological, and social in nature and require that the individual learn to cope with the demands of each task. They typically occur during a particular life stage and should be accomplished satisfactorily at that time for the individual's happiness and success in succeeding tasks.

Havighurst emphasized the teachable moment that occurs when physiological, sociological, and psychological conditions are right and the learner is in a readiness status. Just as there is a favorable time for children to learn to read, so is there a favorable time for older adults to learn to retire.

For the later maturity period, which Havighurst identified as 60+, the following developmental tasks must be mastered: adjusting to retirement, adjusting to declining health and strength, becoming affiliated with late-adult age groups, establishing satisfactory living arrangements, adjusting to the death of a spouse, and maintaining integrity. These developmental tasks differ from those of earlier stages; they tend to reflect a defensive approach to life.

Other researchers have studied the developmental stages of adults. Levinson (11) examined the life stages of 40 middle-aged men selected from various types of work: hourly employees, business executives, academic biologists, and novelists. He reported his findings in a book titled *The Seasons of a Man's Life*. His model focuses on the "individual life structure," which consists of a series of stable and transitional stages. The stable stages last 8–10 years each in which the individual builds, modifies, and rebuilds his life structure. The transitional intervals last 3–4 years each. During these times the individual is shifting from one life stage to another. Levinson described major life periods as eras and identified them as childhood and adolescence, early adulthood, middle adulthood, and late adulthood. The transition intervals he labeled early adult, midlife, and later adult.

Like Havighurst, Levinson (11) stressed the importance of accomplishing certain developmental tasks at each life stage. During the early adult era (22–40 years), individuals explore the various possibilities for adult living and develop their own stable life structure. In the early 20s, they formulate a dream, which pictures the lifestyle they want to have, particularly in terms of marriage and career. In this era, individuals define their goals, find a mentor, enter a vocation, and develop new intimate relationships.

About age 30, young adults either accept the choices made earlier or try new directions. About age 40, according to Levinson, people face a major crisis. The developmental tasks of this midlife transition include appraising and leaving the early adult stage; deciding on a new life structure for middle adulthood; and dealing with major polarities of life such as, young/old, destructive/creative, masculine/feminine, and attachment/separation. This is the time when individuals may realize that their "dream" (or goal) will never be attained or that it has not produced the hoped-for sense of satisfaction. The strong commitment given to career during the early adult era is seriously questioned in midlife and higher priorities are assigned to family and friends. This is the time when individuals construct a revised future that takes growing older into consideration. Levinson's study stops at about age 65.

Roger Gould (12) reported his research on adults in his book, *Transformations*. Several of his conclusions are noteworthy. First, adulthood is a time of growth and change. Second, individual growth is "the release from arbitrary internal constraints" (p. 321); it is a process of liberation. Third, midlife (ages 35–45) "is every bit as turbulent as adolescence, except we can use all this striving to blend a healthier, happier life" (p. 307).

Gould proposed seven stages of adult life (13):

1 16–18: desire to escape parental dominance;
2 18–22: substitutes friends for family;
3 22–28: commitment to a career and to children;
4 29–34: questioning self and role, vulnerable to dissatisfaction with career and marriage;
5 35–43: urgency to attain goals, aware of time limitations, shifting goals;
6 43–50: accepting one's status, more inner-directedness;
7 50–60: mellowing of feelings and relationships, death a new pressure, concern with time and health.

Gould's view of adult life appears to be a slowing down in the late 40s and the 50s.

Gail Sheehy in her book *Passages* (14) described characteristics of the life cycle during the earlier adult years, beginning with "pulling up roots" after age 18. Individuals in the "trying twenties" are preoccupied with the externals of life and forming a life pattern. The 30s are a stage when young adults put down roots and attempt to establish career and family life. Sheehy saw the period from the mid-30s to the mid-40s as the "Deadline Decade" when individuals become aware of the loss of youth and wonder where they are going. During the mid-40s, equilibrium is regained and a new stability is achieved. This is a time of renewal or resignation (14, pp. 37–46).

Although her discussion of the life cycle does not extend beyond age 50, Sheehy emphasized the importance of courage to let go of each stage and to find new responses that will release the satisfactions of the next stage. She reminded her readers that "the power to animate all of life's seasons is a power that resides within us" (14, p. 514).

All of these adult development theorists suggest that individuals have the capacity or potential for growth. However, it is interesting to note that most of them do not carry their stages of human development beyond age 55 or 65. Erikson (9), for example, described four of his seven life stages as associated with childhood and adolescence and only one with late adulthood. Even when later maturity is included, most theorists have failed to emphasize the positive growth potential of the later years. Havighurst (10), for example, focused most of the developmental tasks of late adulthood on adjustment to decline and loss.

In addition to identifying successive stages of development over the life span, Levinson (11) identified four major periods of life, as noted above. Other theorists reduced these periods to three: early, middle, and late. The French labeled the late adult period as "le troisieme age," the experiencing of which gives fuller meaning to the other two.

Lowenthal (15) suggested that older persons react to their losses in later life in one of several ways. Some limit their goals and behaviors, disengaging themselves from an active lifestyle. Others meet losses by taking on new roles and relationships, a pattern which she called "transcendence" (5, p. 441). Gresham (16) described his own life experience as a series of renewals or surges of energy appropriate to particular life stages. He referred to Carl Jung's opinion that persons in later life find within themselves those qualities of meaning that persons in early adulthood seek in the world around them (16, p. 19).

The point is, of course, that late adulthood has much to offer those persons who include this period of life in their perception of the life span as a totality of human experience and who plan for this period through setting appropriate goals and preparing themselves to achieve these goals. If this third period provides the opportunity for discovering and enriching the fuller meanings of the first two, older persons have a strong reason for making the most of this period of their lives. The process of life development then reaches fruition in later life. For those persons who believe in life after death, the event of death represents just another step in their own personal development.

TRANSITION PERIODS

Special attention needs to be given to the periods of transition occurring between the various life stages, as described by Levinson and others. These are periods marked by change, transformation, or perhaps even crisis in the life patterns of individuals.

These periods tend to occur as individuals complete the developmental tasks of one life stage and find themselves faced with a new set of tasks appropriate to the next stage. Such changes can arouse feelings of uncertainty, uneasiness, even fear.

Various external events may trigger transition periods, such as marriage, new employment, or the loss of one's spouse. In addition, certain nonevents may give rise to life changes for individuals, such as wedding plans failing to materialize or the prospective buyer of one's business withdrawing an offer to purchase.

Schlossberg (17) recognized the potential impact of transition periods on adult development in her book *Counseling Adults in Transition*. She developed a detailed analysis of these periods which helps to clarify for counselors the many elements involved and the various points for possible intervention and offering assistance (17).

Elements of her analysis are the transition event itself, the individual and his or her characteristics and resources, and the social environment, including the individual's social network.

THE HUMAN POTENTIAL

Combs, Avila, and Purkey have observed that a notable characteristic of human beings is their capabilities, not their limitations. "From everything we can observe, it seems clear that few of us ever remotely approach the potentialities for effective behavior which lie within us" (18, p. 126).

Yet, our society has tended to evaluate capabilities and potentials in more physical terms. From the point of view of physical strength, the conditions of the physical body are most important. However, individuals react most often to the world around them on the basis of their perceptions of the events and conditions of that world, as well as the particular meanings these things have for them. In terms of behaviors, the intellectual and emotional elements of individuals are more important than the physical (18, p. 123).

Rogers believed, on the basis of his long experience as a psychotherapist, that individuals have within themselves the capacity to move toward more mature living. "Whether one calls it a growth tendency, a drive toward self-actualization, or a forward-moving directional tendency, it is the mainspring of life" (19, p. 35). Rogers was also convinced that he, as a psychotherapist, could only provide a quality of relationship from which individuals could discover for themselves their capacity for growth and development.

Missing from many persons' view of retirement, or the third period of their lives, is the realization that individuals can and do continue to grow and develop throughout their lives. The aforementioned developmental theorists and psychologists have emphasized the capacity for growth which individuals have.

For these reasons, a new view of the human life span is needed, one that extends the idea of individual development throughout life.

Figure 1 represents the human life span as having an ascending gradient from life through death to indicate that, in general, individuals have a continuing potential to grow through all stages of life. On the basis of the various developmental theories, this life span is divided into life stages of roughly 7–8 years each, from ages 1 through 100. Between each life stage is a transition or adjustment period of about 3–4 years.

During each life stage certain developmental tasks must be accomplished by individuals before they can progress successfully to the next stage and another set of developmental tasks. This representation includes the life stage of ages 91–100, since more and more persons are now living past their 100th birthday (3). The developmental tasks appropriate to each stage are listed in Table 1 of Chapter 4. Unfortunately some persons do not progress successfully through all stages for various reasons. Thus, they fail to realize their potentials.

Figure 1 also suggests that the human life span is roughly divided into three periods, early, middle, and later. The late 20s and early 30s, along with the late 60s and early 70s, are possible times of special stress because individuals within these stages often realize that they are leaving one major period of life and are moving into another, which represents an unknown and is therefore to be feared. Individuals going through these stress periods may need the support of family, close friends, or trained counselors.

LIFE ARENAS

Another way to understand the life process and human development is to identify the major arenas within which individuals operate. These have been variously defined as family, career, leisure, intimacy, and inner life (20). Individuals tend to concentrate more or less of their attention in one or more of these arenas at different stages in their lives; at some stages, they may be active in all arenas at roughly the same time.

Problems encountered in one arena are likely to carry over into others. For example, marital discord in the family arena probably will adversely affect behaviors in the career arena, and, conversely, job dissatisfaction in the career arena will probably have an impact within the family arena. However, the individual's difficulty or lack of experience in coping with relationships within the intimacy arena may have led to the marital discord in the family arena. The root of this individual's problems in the family and career arenas would really be found in the intimacy arena.

The arena concept can be an excellent means for both older and younger persons to discover why their development at various stages is not progressing satisfactorily. In addition, this concept can help individuals to initiate corrective

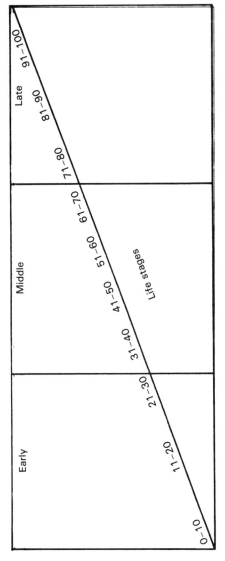

Figure 1 Human Life Span. Life stages are roughly 1–8 years each, with transition periods of 3–4 years between each stage. Transition periods are not shown in this figure for simplification purposes. Stages and transition intervals are obviously variable for individuals.

action. Building on Levinson's (11) idea of life structure, Johnson has devised a model in which the life arenas are the component parts of life structure (20).

Career Arena

Schlossberg (21) described the career arena as one of prime significance to most adults because work is central to an individual's life structure. Work determines one's direction, activities, friendships, self-esteem, and self-concept.

The stereotype of career has been that the individual chooses an occupation early in life, after high school or college, and stays with that occupation until retirement. This situation is no longer true, for at least two reasons: First, economic conditions have favored job mobility; second, rapid advances in technology have not only greatly increased the types of jobs available but also have made many jobs obsolete. Job retraining has often become a necessary option.

Retirement from full-time employment was a new development in the world of work during the 20th century. Encouraging individuals to leave their jobs at age 65 was promoted by federal government agencies and labor unions as a means of opening up job opportunities for younger people. Gradually, retirement was accepted as part of the occupational cycle.

Currently, changes seem to be occurring in the popular concepts of career. Rather than envisioning career as one job for a lifetime, people are talking about "serial" careers, one often very different from earlier ones. There are several reasons for this trend toward serial careers: Not only are some existing jobs disappearing, but also workers often are finding their jobs and job settings personally dissatisfying. In addition, the U.S. supply of workers is shrinking so that more older persons are being encouraged to remain at work. This situation is changing the traditional concept of retirement.

People are living longer, to the point that the number of their working years and the number of their retirement years are becoming roughly the same. How shall the time in retirement be spent? Neither individuals nor our society has clearly formulated answers to this question. Obvious answers include working longer in the same career field, although perhaps part-time; finding a new and hopefully stimulating "second" career; entering community services, probably as a volunteer; embarking upon one or more leisure interests; or combining one or more of these possibilities. The special features of activities in the so-called retirement period are choices that are based on personal preferences and more flexible time schedules.

A review of these alternatives suggests that in the foreseeable future, retirement, as it has been understood, will cease to exist for large numbers of people. Instead, individuals will view their lives as a series of developmental stages, with renewal checkpoints for evaluation and refocusing of goals.

Family Arena

The family has been, and still is, vital to the psychosocial well-being of its members. It provides support in the sense of both protection and also accommodation to the society of which it is a part. The family gives to its members a sense of identity, a sense of belonging, and a sense of separateness (22). But the family as a social unit is changing, as society is changing.

Some of its functions have been taken over by other social institutions. The education of younger members is largely accomplished by the schools, the communications media, peers, and, in the case of the very young, day-care centers. The older members find themselves living apart in original family homes, retirement communities for older persons, adult congregate living facilities, day-care centers, or nursing homes. For the adult children, family roles have often changed, with both working full time and sometimes sharing roles once assumed by the man or woman. Economic pressures have combined to force the adult children to work full time in order to maintain their accustomed lifestyle. The total impact of changes in contemporary society has been to direct family life outward and away from itself.

One of the consequences of social change has been a weakening of the sense of belonging once provided by the family. A difficulty experienced by family members is often the gap between their expectations of the family unit and their experiences of its reality. Problems of adjustment and adaptation thus occur. Some people no longer have a clear understanding of what a family is and what its functions should be. At a meeting of delegates attending the 1980 White House Conference on Families, those present were unable to agree on a definition of the family in America today (personal experience of one of the authors).

According to Minuchin (22), the family is a system that involves various patterns of behavior. These patterns include different levels of authority and certain expectations of each family member. The ability of the system to continue depends on its flexibility.

Obviously, the work and family arenas are closely interrelated. Individuals develop and maintain themselves through their experiences in each. The roles and requirements of each arena change over time. In the family, for example, the early role of sons or daughters is principally that of learning and of accommodating to the wishes of the parent or parents. As the parents and children age, their relationship roles change greatly. The functions of the adult children become much like those of the parents, while the functions of the parents become similar to those once carried out by their children. Taking these roles and functions is often equally difficult for the parents and their adult children. Successful adjustment to these changes is based on mutual respect and recognition of the developmental tasks of the later period of life (23).

Intimacy Arena

The intimacy arena includes the wide range of relationships that individuals experience with others. They are marked by openness, trust, and disclosure. These relationships may be at the intellectual, physical, or emotional levels. Erikson (9) believed that individuals must first achieve personal stability through establishing their own self-identity, before they can safely blend their identities with those of others. He described intimacy as the capacity "to commit [oneself] to concrete affiliations and partnerships and to develop the ethical strength to abide by such commitments, even though they may call for significant sacrifices and compromises" (9, p. 263).

Intimacy is the sharing of oneself with others; it involves the capacity to self-disclose. The ability to do so emerges at an early age and continues to develop during the life span. At first, the willingness to share oneself and express love may be stressful. But as individuals mature and become more confident of themselves, they can enter into relationships that are more open and honest. Intimacy determines their capacity to establish and maintain meaningful relationships with other persons. These persons include acquaintances, friends, family members, and marital partners.

The sharing of oneself with another person who is also willing to share establishes greater personal confidence and personal satisfaction in both. This sharing presupposes a high regard of oneself as well as of others in the formation of an intimate, interpersonal relationship with another human being. If the capacity for intimacy remains undeveloped or underdeveloped, individuals may find themselves isolated, avoiding deeper contact with others, absorbed in themselves, or unable to establish meaningful relationships with others.

At various stages of life, the formation of intimate relationships is a critical issue. As young persons move toward adulthood, such relationships serve to encourage independence and to weaken ties with their families of origin. During the adult years, experiencing intimacy can lead to renewed interest in oneself and one's spouse. For older persons, intimate relationships can foster feelings of life satisfaction and well-being.

In each major life period certain developmental tasks must be accomplished again. Sharpening attitudes and skills involved in expressing intimacy is one such task. The task is similar at each life period, yet there are differences. These differences can arise out of the confusion individuals may experience regarding their own feelings, goals, and directions, as well as from ambiguities they sense in the world around them. In the case of older persons, uncertainties about themselves, about their relationships with others, and about the expectations of the society in which they live can all be factors that inhibit their growth as human beings, especially in the intimacy arena.

For example, one significant expression of intimacy is through sexual relations. However, present social stereotypes place intercourse off limits for older persons (24). Yet, for those whose sexual activity has been satisfying during earlier years, there are no physiological reasons why it should not be continued during later years (25, p. 10). In fact, sexual activity can contribute to the health and sense of well-being of persons in later life (25, p. 9).

Intimacy, as an ability and skill, influences the quality of the individual's communication with others. This quality includes openness, satisfaction with self, and acceptance of the other person. It enables the individual to listen with understanding, to be able to appreciate the other person's points of view. The capacity for intimacy carries over into the other life arenas. In fact, success or failure in the other arenas may often be attributed to the individual's stage of development in the intimacy arena. The ability to expand personal relationships during retirement is often influenced by the individual's experiences in the intimacy arena.

Inner Life Arena

Whereas intimacy concerns relationships outside the individual, the inner life arena concerns relationships within the self. Those relationships involve the individual's concept of self and of his or her physical body. Also involved is the person's spiritual self and concepts of a higher power, whatever that power may be, which helps to answer questions about the meaning of life and its ultimate purpose. The inner life arena embraces the person's emotional, physical, and spiritual life. It affects all aspects of his or her external world. The ability to look at oneself and to value one's internal processes is essential to a healthier, happier life.

However, this arena is marked by complexities and difficulties. Foremost, perhaps, is the willingness to place oneself at the top of one's value list and to give the time required to sort out needs, interests, and priorities. Competing for attention are those interests growing out of the intellectual, material, and spiritual elements of one's inner life. Time is needed for introspection and contemplation—activities that are often avoided by many persons. The other life arenas seem easier to address, in some ways, so that this arena is often neglected, even though it is central to one's successful growth and development. Formulation of one's life goals and reasonable understanding of one's competing interests and preferences give guidance and support to activities in the other life arenas.

The individual's concept of self is built on experiences and dreams. Experiences and behaviors form the self as it actually is; dreams form the basis of what the individual would like to be. If there is a marked discrepancy between the real and ideal self, the individual is likely to have feelings of guilt, discouragement, depression, and despair. The self-concept involves the thinking self, which helps to set personal goals and establish personal values. This part of the self evaluates the quality of the various roles taken in the other life arenas. Self-concept and one's value system are considered in more detail in Chapter 4.

Concepts of a healthy physical self provide the person with a sense of physical vigor, which in turn creates a feeling of general well-being. Satisfaction with the conditions of the physical body leads to good feelings in the intellectual, emotional, and spiritual spheres. It is important to remember that the physical, intellectual, emotional, and spiritual elements of the person are intimately interrelated. The ideal situation is a balance among all four.

The spiritual self is concerned with the individual's value system: In what does the person believe and what standards govern attitudes and behavior? A value system develops over a person's lifetime and is derived from many sources: family, friends, business associates, and communications media, including books, magazines, newspapers, radio, and television. Information from all of these sources is filtered through the person's goals, roles, and preferences and form his or her value system.

For a great many persons this information is sorted, and accepted or rejected, through a religious and/or philosophical screen created by experiences with a religious creed and/or body of thought. This screen helps determine for the person standards of right or wrong to apply to behavior. The spiritual self attempts to answer such questions as "Who am I?" and "What is the purpose of my being on this earth?" A person's values, held in the early part of life, are likely to be replaced by values developed in later life. For example, a question in early life may be "Who am I in relation to others?" In later life the question may be "Who am I in relation to my Supreme Being?"

During earlier years, a primary value for men may be physical strength; for women it may be physical beauty. In later years, these values tend to shift to those focusing on the intellectual and the spiritual elements of life. When such a shift does not occur, unhappiness is likely to result. Concern for the physical values should remain, but not in a primary position.

The spiritual element of one's inner life tends to increase in importance as individuals grow older. For some, this element becomes central as they deal with the issues of purpose and meaning in their lives. It can contribute to positive feelings of trust in themselves and in a higher power to undergird the activities of their daily lives. It can do much to replace fear of death with acceptance of its inevitability. Not all persons find the spiritual element as helpful; some redefine it, and others rely more on other philosophical approaches.

Leisure Arena

The leisure arena is often misunderstood as referring to activities which represent a waste of time and dissipate resources. For some people, leisure is the opposite of work and therefore nonproductive. More and more people are seeing leisure as parallel to work and equally necessary for the well-being of the whole person, perhaps even more necessary (4).

Leisure is actually difficult to define because it is inevitably compared with work. Perhaps the best way to think about leisure is to describe it as an attitude of mind and what it can do for an individual. Basically, leisure has no external constraints on the use of time, and its direction is controlled from within the person. Its functions are relaxation, entertainment, and personal development.

Like work, leisure is activity; it can be the means for developing feelings of self-worth, social status, and personal potential. It can lead to self-discovery and a better quality of life. Leisure activities represent a continuum, from relaxation to diversion, to development, to creativity, to sensual transcendence.

The Greeks emphasized contemplation and activity for its own sake. The Romans viewed leisure in terms of rest and recreation. The Chinese saw leisure as an experience of immortality. Nineteenth century Americans found life to be work oriented or family centered, with little time for recreation or rest. When there was no longer work or family, life lost its meaning. The joy of living for its own sake has received a new emphasis in the 20th century as a result of the various technologies that have made more non-job-related time available to more people. Social forces are producing radically different lifestyles for Americans in which work, in the conventional sense, takes less and less time and therefore is relatively less important as a consumer of time or a focus of energy.

The leisure problems for many older Americans are (a) coping with the amount of time available to them, (b) seeing leisure activities as opportunities for self-development, and (c) overcoming the lifelong belief that only work activities have real meaning (26). Often, real issues are the right to feel happy, and what is happiness anyway?

Happiness means different things to different people. Philosophers define happiness in various ways. One says it is freedom from pain; another finds it in the achieving of something rather than in the possessing of it. Happiness involves caring for and sharing with others. A contemporary executive says happiness is using all of one's abilities for goals in which one believes. Some writers associate happiness with joy inside the self. We give ourselves permission to be happy, to have a positive approach to life and living. Some people keep looking for happiness outside themselves; they are most likely to find it inside themselves.

The use of leisure activities often brings people in tune with themselves, because the selection of these activities and the amount of time given to them are very personal choices. Basically, individuals decide what leisure activities they enjoy doing and do them, without being required to do so by others.

Better understanding of the various life arenas in which they take part enables individuals to understand themselves better and the advantages of achieving a reasonable balance among these arenas. Such an understanding also helps individuals set realistic goals for their own happiness. Helpful also is gaining an understanding of changes occurring in the environment and adapting to these changes.

IMPACT OF CHANGE

A big problem of the human environment, both now and in the near future, is the fact of change and the rapidity of change. In the recent past, change was sufficiently gradual that parents could help children to understand and adapt to the environment that parents had experienced and children were experiencing. This situation is no longer true. Change is now so rapid that the world being experienced by children is very different from that experienced by their parents. One result is the alienation of parents and children who do not understand each others' viewpoints.

What are some of the effects of rapid change on the people of today, and especially older people? The first is the lack of information and experience in adapting to changing conditions. The second is that individuals in a changing world are not sure of who they are and what their roles in families, communities, and the larger world are. Being unclear about one's identity or roles creates a sense of powerlessness and an inability to determine personal directions. The third effect of rapid change is that today's world has become both tiny and immense: tiny in the sense that a computer chip can store more knowledge than a library; immense in the sense that scientists have discovered a quasar described as 20 billion light years from earth.

Whereas the pace of changes in the environment has speeded up, the ability of older persons to comprehend and adapt to these changes has tended to slow down, partially, at least, because older persons have neglected to maintain a breadth of knowledge base or to exercise sufficiently their mental and physical processes.

DIRECTIONS OF FUTURE CHANGE

In order to live more effectively in a world of change, individuals should become more knowledgeable about the directions of change. Sources of this kind of information include forecasts of the future to be found in a various places, such as publications like *The Futurist* (27). Major areas of change to investigate include population trends; family size and configurations; the structure and methods of education, including lifelong learning; technological growth in such specialties as communications methods, computers, and automation; types of work and working conditions; maintaining health, what it will cost, and who will pay; the business world and the state of the economy; the environment and world resources; and the interdependence of countries and continents.

What can be learned from studying these large-scale areas of change? People will discover that the familiar is being replaced by the unfamiliar and new; the new requires different attitudes and different behaviors. Whereas there is much discussion of developments in material things, little is mentioned in specific terms about the resulting need for development of the human potential to cope with change.

Consideration of the magnitude of change in today's world brings with it two obvious conclusions: Individuals must remain informed, and they must enlarge their capacity for adapting personally to changes. Another advantage for increasing their knowledge of changing conditions is that individuals will be better prepared to plan alternative courses of action for their own futures.

IMPLICATIONS FOR COUNSELORS

We suggest that in addition to gaining competency in the use of techniques to help clients, counselors need to develop knowledge and understanding in key areas involving clients and their behavior. One area is certainly the life process viewed as a totality, with each life stage building on the ones before and each succeeding stage influenced by earlier ones. This life process takes on added meaning when it is understood as developmental and that each person has the potential to grow from stage to stage. This understanding is especially important for effective counseling with older clients. It involves not only counselors' goals but also counselors' attitudes. Counselors cannot forget that age bias is likely to affect adversely their work with older clients.

Another important area is the concept of life arenas, with client experiences in one affecting those in one or more others, depending on the importance placed by the client on a particular arena. For a client to achieve balance in activities within each of the five life arenas is a highly desirable goal. In actuality, such a balance is not often reached, leading to relationship problems for many clients. To help clients with these and other problems, counselors must explore existing conditions in each of their life arenas.

Particular attention should be given to the intimacy and leisure arenas. The sharing of themselves with another sometimes proves very difficult, especially if clients have some negative views of themselves. In the case of older clients, sharing of self may have been regarded as undesirable according to family tradition. This tradition may also have placed leisure in an unacceptable category. Counselors may have a twofold responsibility in the leisure arena: They may need to understand it as a positive and unique activity, with values in and of itself; and they may have to educate their clients, especially older clients, in the meaning and uses of leisure.

A third important area involving clients, regardless of age, is major categories of change in the worlds of today and tomorrow, and the possible impact of change on individuals in their life planning. Counselors should think in terms of the future for their clients, not only through obtaining information about future scenarios but also in thinking about the possible impact of future developments on their lives and behaviors. It should be remembered that older, as well as younger, people have developing futures that necessitate setting realistic goals and assessing resources needed to reach them. This fact is important for older clients as well as for counselors to understand and act on.

GROUP ACTIVITIES

Divide participants into groups of six or eight to provide an opportunity for individual members to share their reactions with others. Have group members respond to the following suggested discussion questions listed under major topics found in this chapter:

1. Living as a process:
   (a) Where do I think I am in the life process?
   (b) What is one of my goals which guides my actions right now?
   (c) How does having a goal make me feel? Or, how does not having a goal make me feel?
2. Exploring life arenas:
   (a) Which of the five life arenas has been the most important in my life? Why?
   (b) Which of the life arenas is most important to me now? Why?
   (c) Which of the five life arenas has been least important in my life? Why?
   (d) Which of the life arenas is least important to me now? Why?
3. Anticipating change:
   (a) What are some of the changes occurring in today's world that might affect me the most?
   (b) What are some of the major changes in the world that have *really* affected my life and my way of living?
   (c) How do I react to change? What are several examples of my reactions?

Discuss with the total group (all participants) general reactions to this exercise.

REFERENCES

1 Barfield, R. E., & Morgan, J. N. (1978). Trends in satisfaction with retirement. *The Gerontologist, 18*(1), 19–23.
2 Lowry, J. H. (1985). Predictors of successful aging in retirement. In E. B. Palmore (Ed.), *Normal Aging III* (pp. 394–404). Durham, NC: Duke University Press.
3 Ekerdt, D. I. (1986). The busy ethic: Moral continuity between work and retirement. *The Gerontologist, 26*(3), 243–294.
4 McDaniels, C. (1982). *Leisure: Integrating a neglected component in life planning.* Columbus, OH: National Center for Research in Vocational Education.

 5 Stevens-Long, J. (1982). *Adult life, developmental process.* (2nd ed.). Palo Alto, CA: Mayfield.
 6 Roser, B., & Jerdee, T. H. (1985). *Older employees: New roles for valued resources.* Homewood, KY: Dow-Jones.
 7 Lugo, J. V., & Hershey, G. L. (1979). *Human development.* New York: Macmillan.
 8 Harris, L., & Associates. (1975). *The myth and reality of aging in America.* Washington, DC: National Council on the Aging.
 9 Erikson, E. H. (1963). *Childhood and society.* New York: Norton.
10 Havighurst, R. J. (1972). *Developmental tasks and education.* (3rd ed.). New York: McKay.
11 Levinson, D. (1978). *The seasons of a man's life.* New York: Knopf.
12 Gould, R. L. (1978). *Transformations.* New York: Simon and Schuster.
13 Gould, R. L. (1975). Adult life stages, growth toward self tolerance. *Psychology Today, 8,* 74–78.
14 Sheehy, G. (1977). *Passages.* New York: E. P. Dutton.
15 Lowenthal, J. F., Thurnker, M., & Cheroboga, D. (1976). *Four stages of life.* San Francisco: Jossey-Bass.
16 Gresham, P. E. (1980). *With wings as eagles.* Winter Park, FL: Anna.
17 Schlossberg, N. K. (1984). *Counseling adults in transition.* New York: Springer.
18 Combs, A. W., Avila, D. L., & Purkey, W. W. (1971). *Helping relationships.* Boston: Allyn and Bacon.
19 Rogers, C. R. (1961). *On becoming a person.* Boston: Houghton Mifflin.
20 Johnson, R. P. (1984). Midlife lifestyles. *Midlife Wellness, 2,* 4–10.
21 Schlossberg, N. K., Troll, L. E., & Leibowitz, Z. (1978). *Perspectives on counseling adults: Issues and skills.* Monterey, CA: Brooks/Cole.
22 Minuchin, S. (1974). *Families and family therapy.* Boston: Harvard University Press.
23 Myers, J. E. (1989). *Adult children and aging parents.* Alexandria, VA: American Association for Counseling and Development.
24 Kennedy, C. E. (1978). *Human development: The adult years and aging.* New York: Macmillan.
25 Butler, R. N., & Lewis, M. I. (1976). *Sex after sixty.* New York: Harper and Row.
26 Myers, J. E. (1984). Leisure counseling for older persons. In E. T. Dowd (Ed.), *Leisure counseling: Concepts and applications* (pp. 157–177). Springfield, IL: C. C. Thomas.
27 *The Futurist.* (Available from the World Future Society, 4916 St. Elmo Avenue, Bethesda, Maryland, 20814).

Chapter Three

Role of the Counselor

The counselor can be of tremendous assistance and support to those older persons in the process of adapting to social and technological change and/or determining directions for the later, significant part of their lives. Counselors are concerned not just with the solving of problems but also with the further development of potential. To be most effective, counselors must see the present life experience of older clients as part of a total life process.

Counseling has been defined in a variety of ways by any number of publics. Some confusion exists over what it actually is; however, counseling usually is referred to as an art and seldom as a science. It consists of helping interactions between a trained helper and a person needing assistance, a helpee. In the broadest sense, virtually any profession or activity using verbal interaction is able to refer to some component of its service as "counseling."

Persons today may receive legal counseling, beauty counseling, insurance counseling, financial counseling, or genetic counseling, to name a few. Guidance counseling, long the domain of school counselors, often is viewed in terms of paperwork and scheduling functions. Thus, counseling seems to be a generic term with wide application. Clearly, it is necessary to define the term within the context of retirement issues.

This chapter begins with an attempt to answer the question "What is counseling?" Counseling goals are then explored, along with the variety of possible roles for counselors, particularly counselors working with midlife and older persons. The knowledge and skills necessary for counselors to implement these goals and roles are discussed, followed by implications for counselors.

WHAT IS COUNSELING?

Counseling is a special kind of helping relationship involving at least two persons, hereafter referred to as counselor and client. It is distinguished from other types of helping relationships not only by the nature of these two persons, but also by the focus of their interactions.

Counselors may be trained as professionals or paraprofessionals. Professional counselors begin employment with a minimum of a master's degree. Current national standards require a minimum 2-year entry-level degree program. Many have more advanced training, including doctoral preparation. Supervised clinical work experience is an integral part of professional training programs. Paraprofessional counselors usually obtain a minimum of 20–30 hr of training in basic communication and referral skills. No standards exist for paraprofessional certification. National certification is available for professional counselors, as well as licensure in about one-half of the states.

The training of counselors is similar to and overlaps that of psychologists, who in turn receive clinical training not unlike that of psychiatrists. The latter have medical degrees and the ability to prescribe medications. Most psychiatrists are trained in psychoanalytic methods and focus their treatment on severely impaired populations (e.g., psychotic and neurotic individuals, persons with personality disorders or mental illnesses). The scope of practice of psychologists overlaps that of psychiatrists, with a focus on treatment of personality disorders and neuroses. Psychologists and counselors also share commonalities in treatment populations.

Increasingly, professional counselors are being referred to as "mental health counselors," to distinguish them from legal or other advisers, and to reflect the major focus of their work. Mental health counselors seek to encourage and promote good mental health. Their orientation is not so much to treating significant psychopathology, though many are trained to do so, but rather toward facilitating coping with "the human condition"—those situations, issues, and problems that confront persons in the day-to-day process of living. It has been said that counselors work with "normal" people with "normal" problems.

Following this line of reasoning, clients may be defined as more or less "normal" individuals. Their concerns encompass and involve each of the major domains or arenas of functioning described in Chapter 2: work, family, leisure, intimacy, and inner life. These arenas are not mutually exclusive but rather overlap and interact. Change in one arena reflects and may cause changes in other arenas. Each individual must approach life holistically, encompassing all domains. In the same vein, effective counselors must consider all aspects of their clients' lives and circumstances.

The focus of counseling, then, is a holistic approach to helping people meet the "normal" demands of living. Part of this approach relates to developmental issues, or general tendencies for growth and development over the life span. Certain specific issues or tasks confront persons at certain times in their lives. Often referred to as "normative" developmental issues and/or transitions, the various challenges to growth over the life span can present persistent and demanding requirements for coping and adaptation.

For example, Havighurst (1) described one of the major developmental tasks of late maturity as "adjusting to retirement and reduced income." At least the first part of that adjustment is so significant as to generate an entire book for helping people cope! The same may be said for each of the life stages, life tasks, and transitions identified by numerous developmental theorists. When the uniquenesses of each person and situation are considered in addition to the normative aspects of development, the enormous task facing counselors—the mental health variety—becomes apparent.

In order to meet the broad array of needs of potential clients, counselors must be prepared to approach them as individuals; jointly with the clients assess their unique circumstances and needs; and plan, implement, and evaluate treatment strategies. As persons grow older they become more like themselves and less like anyone else. Consequently, there are increasing needs for individualized treatment approaches.

Sherman (2) addressed these needs through a model described as "integrative counseling," an "eclectic approach designed specifically for work with older adults. It includes a method of assessment, a differential treatment model based on type of problem and time factors, and a repertoire of techniques consistent with its treatment model (p. 2)." The integrative approach is designed to identify and, importantly, to enhance the normal development of persons in later adulthood. The focus on positive mental health is reflected in attempts to describe and use the strengths and resources of clients that develop in the course of living over many years.

The integrative approach begins with assessment or problem identification and incorporates a continuum of treatment. The four phases of the continuum are: (a) provision of necessary services, materials, and/or support to meet the immediate situation; (b) provision of support and encouragement of coping to effect self-esteem and morale; (c) encouragement of an increasingly internal locus of control wherein the individual assumes responsibility for his or her decisions and actions; and (d) provision of services to effect positive changes in self-concept and self-esteem. Persons who feel good about themselves and confident in their abilities, that is, those who are mentally healthy, are able to make decisions and choices that enable them to meet and sustain their needs. Integrative counseling aims to facilitate mentally healthy lifestyles.

Within the integrative model, the variety of problems and issues faced by adults and especially older adults may be addressed. The entire repertoire of counseling skills and techniques may be employed, based on any one or more theoretical approaches. The model may be applied in individual, family, and/or group counseling, and may incorporate functions ranging from education to therapy. The nature of counseling may be further clarified by an examination of counseling goals.

COUNSELING GOALS

As is true of counseling in general, counseling goals may be described from a variety of perspectives. One overall goal already has been stated: helping "normal" individuals cope with normative issues, concerns, and situations. Within that broad goal, Johnson and Riker (3) identified seven primary goals for gerontological counselors. These include:

> *Problem resolution:* counseling aimed at assisting persons in solving problems that they are unable to solve themselves;
> *Behavioral change:* counseling aimed at a redirection of typical responses to frustrations or encouragement of different attitudes toward other people or self;
> *Decision making:* counseling aimed at stimulating the individual to evaluate, make, accept, and act on his or her own choice;
> *Positive mental health:* counseling aimed at behavioral integration, adjustment, positive identification with others, acceptance of responsibility, and independence;
> *Personal effectiveness:* counseling aimed at enabling persons to thrive and not merely survive;
> *Knowledge of the aging process and its effects:* counseling aimed at awareness, knowledge of age-related changes, self-acceptance, and striving for optimal functioning within the limitations imposed by aging;
> *Self-advocacy:* counseling aimed at developing self-advocacy techniques and actions, including information about and referral to governmental or other community agencies.

These goals were evaluated by a group of 41 gerontological counseling experts and a sample of directors of area agencies on aging. (Area agencies, an integral part of the aging network, are described in the last section of this chapter.) Each counselor was asked to rate the goals on a 7-point Likert scale. A summary of the resulting data is provided in Table 1. As can be seen from Table 1, counselors ranked positive mental health as the primary goal of counseling and enhancing personal effectiveness as second. Counselors ascribed least impor-

Table 1   Gerontological Counseling Goals as Viewed by Counselors and Area Agency on Aging (AAA) Directors

Gerontological counseling goals	Counselors			AAA directors rank
	M	SD	Rank	
Problem resolution	6.10	1.04	5	1
Behavioral change	6.95	.99	6	7
Decision making	6.29	.98	3	4
Positive mental health	6.61	.77	1	5
Personal effectiveness	6.61	.83	2	3
Knowledge of the aging process	6.20	1.04	4	6
Self-advocacy	5.75	1.12	7	2

tance to behavioral change and self-advocacy. Area agency on aging directors, on the other hand, ascribed most importance to problem resolution and self-advocacy and least importance to knowledge of the aging process and behavioral change.

Clearly, professionally trained counselors seek to affect first and foremost the mental health of their clients. Within the integrative model, positive mental health is viewed as a key element. Persons who perceive themselves as healthy and in control of their lives are more able to resolve their own problems, advocate for their own needs, and implement behavioral changes necessary for effective living. The goals of counseling extend beyond more effective living, however. Counselors seek also to help individuals to reach their maximum potential in all the arenas. Stated another way, counselors aim to facilitate self-actualization, a process that has been defined in several ways.

Self-actualization, a term originally used by Maslow (4), referred to the human capacity and potential to *become* all that one is capable of being. Maslow considered that all persons are born with the innate potential to self-actualize and that the process would invariably happen if persons were permitted enough latitude for behaviors. The self-actualized person has more efficient reality perception; freshness of appreciation; autonomy; a democratic philosophy, including respect and reverence for the uniqueness of others; and a belief in something greater than oneself. Self-actualizing persons are capable of living life fully, and of having peak experiences.

Combs (5), in discussing the "adequate person," indicated that people are far more capable of "becoming" than once was widely believed. He included that potentials can be created and that counselors can encourage persons to be self-directed, have positive self-concepts, and be open to experience based on having a sense of inner security.

Another view was provided by Bonner (6), who wrote about the "proactive person." This individual is one who is free to make his or her own decisions, has an aesthetic view of life, is idealistic and creative, and is capable of self-transformation. Bonner's proactive person has developed forward movements in a variety of life situations and to a very high degree.

A final definition is provided by Carl Rogers (7), who wrote about the "fully functioning person." According to Roger, healthy persons are aware of their attitudes and feelings and are open and willing to trust and accept themselves and their experiences. The healthy person has self-reliance and a willingness to continue to grow and change.

As persons mature and reach retirement age, their potential to function in self-actualizing ways tends to increase. Often, however, this potential is affected by tangible life circumstances and needs, such as finances, health, housing, and work/leisure options. Helping persons make and effect choices to address these circumstances in positive ways thus becomes a major goal of counselors.

Although both area agency on aging directors and counselors work toward the same goal of helping older persons retain and attain independence, they do so in different ways. As shown in Table 1, counselors help persons through facilitating positive mental health and coping strategies, whereas area agency on aging directors work toward the same goal through provision of material services. Both approaches are necessary to enable older persons to become and remain fully functioning persons, setting and achieving goals in each of the five life arenas. It is important for counselors to interact with aging network staff when working with older persons. Potential areas for doing so become more clear when counseling roles are explored.

VARIETY OF ROLES

A variety of roles for gerontological counselors are possible, including both preventive and remedial services. These roles depend to some extent on the setting in which services are provided, which may include anywhere that an older person resides, visits, or otherwise is encountered. Two major studies have been completed to examine gerontological counselor roles. Each of these is discussed below.

Johnson and Riker (3) identified 21 possible roles for gerontological counselors. These roles are listed and defined in Table 2. As can be seen in Table 2, the variety of roles is great. There is no one clear focus of roles; rather, a variety of roles is necessary to meet the array of needs of older individuals in all arenas of life.

Johnson and Riker asked experts in gerontological counseling to rate each role on a 7-point Likert-type Scale according to its value for gerontological counselors. The mean scores for each role are shown in Table 3. Virtually all of the mean scores are high, which is indicative again of the variety of roles that are both possible and important in working with older persons.

Counselors were asked to rank order the roles in terms of their importance for working with older persons, and area agency on aging directors were asked to do the same. The results are shown in Table 3. The highest ranked roles according to the gerontological counselors were preretirement counselor and educator, family counselor, and in-service counselor educator. The lowest ranked roles by this group were financial counselor and manager, services coordinator–services enhancer–client advocate, and employment counselor. Area agency on aging directors indicated the three highest roles as service provider to persons living alone, services coordinator–services enhancer–client advocate, and employment counselor. The three lowest ranked roles by the directors were marital and sex counselor, counselor of the terminally ill, and leisure time counselor. Clearly, there are differences in the perception of counselor roles based on setting and philosophical orientation.

Blake (8) studied the appropriateness of 17 counselor roles and activities in work with older persons. The three most important roles according to this study were family counseling centered around aging-related problems, retirement-related educational or counseling activities with groups and individuals, and training of noncounselors in basic communication and counseling skills (this is identical to the Johnson and Riker role of in-service counselor educator). The three lowest ranked roles were job placement service, housing placement service, and consumer education. Blake's findings were remarkably similar to those of Johnson and Riker (3).

A more recent study by Robison, Comas, Blaas, Kirk, and Freeman (9) examined gerontological counselors in the workplace and the activities they perform. Counselors working in various settings with older persons reported that psychological counseling was the most frequently provided service. This was followed by social and recreational programming; vocational counseling was a distant third. The least often provided services were linking clients with social services, screening eligibility for social services, advocacy and political activities, and direct health care.

Whatever the setting, counselors working with older persons will find themselves called on to perform a variety of roles, depending on the circumstances and needs of the older individuals. At any given time they may be asked

Table 2   Gerontological Counseling Roles

Role	Definition/scope of role
Service provider to persons living alone	Widow support groups, informational services, assertiveness training, communication skills training, support in seeking new social contacts
Bereavement counselor	Empathy and strong emotional support to those mourning a lost loved one
Change agent	Dispel myths about older persons in the community, stimulate positive change in services offered to older persons
Personal counselor	Personal counseling services to those experiencing the effects of aging
Consultant	Process consultation to network agencies, and mental health consultation to professionals (doctors, lawyers, accountants, etc.) dealing with older persons
Specialist in psychological education	Human relations training to those who deal with older persons as well as directly to older person population
Employment counselor	Assisting older persons with their vocational needs and aspirations
Services coordinator–services enhancer–client advocate	Facilitating the proper "services mix" for the individual client, maximizing the quality of services any agency is capable of giving, supportive assistance in expediting services
Financial counselor and manager	Consumer information and support so older persons can maximize their health, housing, and services dollar
In-service counselor–educator	Offering in-service programs to aging network staffs on gerontological issue and techniques in dealing with older persons
Leisure time counselor	Assisting older persons in identifying avocational interests, thereby fostering the meaningful use of time

Table 2   Gerontological Counseling Roles (*Continued*)

Role	Definition/scope of role
Marital and sex counselor	Assisting healthy marital adjustment for older couples, offering accurate information on matters of sexuality
Outreach agent to minorities	Understanding unique problems of Minority older persons and proactively seeking their participation in service programs
Service provider to nursing home and housing complex residents	Helping residents adjust to reality of health problems, communication skills, health care training, time and life review, peer counselor training
Counselor of terminally ill	Assisting those terminally ill in decision making, alternatives scanning, opportunities for personal independence and control
Preretirement counselor and educator	Assisting older persons in making the transition from the work role to the retirement role
Public relations worker	Information to the community to sensitize them to their own aging and the needs of older persons
Gerontological researcher	Conducting local needs assessments, studying counseling strategies, demographic data collecting, etc.
Family counselor	Working with older parents and their adult children to assist both groups in coping with newly emerging problems associated with age
Educational counselor	Assisting older persons in participating in educational opportunities, developing linkages within the community between existing educational resources, and encouraging new educational services
Medical support outreach Counselor	Assisting physicians in giving more comprehensive care to older patients, both in the office and in the home

Table 3   Ratings of Gerontological Counseling Roles by Counselors and Area Agency on Aging (AAA) Directors

Role	Counselors		AAA directors rank
	M	Rank	
Service provider	5.87	9	1
Bereavement counselor	5.85	10	16
Change agent	5.95	8	5
Personal counselor	6.09	4	7
Consultant	6.00	7	12
Specialist in psychological education	6.07	5	8
Employment counselor	5.41	19	3
Services coordinator– services enhancer– client advocate	5.19	20	2
Financial counselor and manager	5.02	21	4
In-service counselor–educator	6.19	3	17
Leisure time counselor	5.63	14	19
Marital and sex counselor	5.65	13	21
Outreach agent to minorities	5.56	16	13
Service provider to nursing home and housing complex residents	5.85	11	6
Counselor of the terminally ill	6.04	6	20
Preretirement counselor and educator	6.41	1	14
Public relations worker	5.56	17	9

Table 3 Ratings of Gerontological Counseling Roles by Counselors and Area Agency on Aging (AAA) Directors (*Continued*)

Role	Counselors		AAA directors rank
	M	Rank	
Gerontological researcher	5.58	12	11
Family counselor	6.37	2	18
Educational counselor	5.62	15	10
Medical support outreach counselor	5.50	18	15

to provide information and referral services and either group or individual counseling with older persons and/or their families. They may need to be friends, supporters, encouragers, and helpers to "normal" individuals dealing with normative issues. They may need to be clinicians prepared to meet the mental health needs of impaired persons and their families. The variety of roles imply an advanced level of knowledge and skill and hence have implications for the training of gerontological counselors.

KNOWLEDGE AND SKILLS OF GERONTOLOGICAL COUNSELORS

Gerontological counselors are first and foremost counselors; therefore, the first requirement for training is that they meet standards applicable to the counseling profession. This means that an entry-level counselor would have a minimum of 2-year master's degree, and a paraprofessional counselor at least 20–30 hr of basic training. The professional counselor would have training in each of the core areas of counselor preparation: foundations of the helping relationship, social and cultural foundations, lifestyle and career development, psychological assessment, group work, human growth and development, professional issues, and research. In addition, supervised work experiences would be completed.

Counselors specializing in work with older persons would need additional training (10). This would include information tailoring each of the core areas listed above to the needs of older persons (11). The first requirement for such counselors would be opportunities to examine and become aware of their own attitudes and values in relation to older persons and the aging process. The adage to "know thyself" is a prerequisite for effective provision of services. Counselors also should become familiar with the prevalent attitudes toward aging held by persons in general, including older persons, and the impact of these attitudes on the lives of older individuals.

Coursework that explores the needs and concerns of older persons now and in the future is essential. The demography of aging, social and psychological aspects of aging, and biological development are important as well. A review of the five life arenas suggests that counselors need to become knowledgeable of issues for older persons related to careers, family, intimacy, inner life, and leisure. Courses may be developed on any of these topics.

A review of the various gerontological counselor roles listed above provides further areas for study. Effectiveness in virtually all of these roles will require the counselor to develop knowledge and information, as well as skills, to meet the specific needs. It will be necessary to become familiar with the broad array of services and programs provided through the Aging Network to facilitate effective and timely referral for needed services (see last section in this chapter for a description of the Aging Network).

Sherman (2), in describing the integrative approach, suggested that counselors for older persons need to sharpen their skills in formal and informal assessment; working with families and groups; and evaluation, planning, and exploring of treatment options. They must learn to build, develop, and use support networks to facilitate positive mental health among their clients.

The study by Robison et al. (9) explored information needs for gerontological counselors in five areas. As shown in Table 4, these information needs were for counseling strategies and techniques, special issues and populations, psychological aspects of aging, consultation/programming, and assessment. For counselors specializing in work with older persons, these topics reflect both common issues and potential deficits in graduate training programs for gerontological counselors.

Attention to the development of skills in counseling is a primary component of all coursework. In addition, counselors choosing to work with older persons will benefit from supervised clinical practice in settings where older persons are found. Feedback from faculty and on-site supervisors will assist trainees to develop sensitivity and skill in meeting the counseling needs of older people (11). Supervised practice ordinarily will occur during the final stages of training, representing an opportunity to apply the knowledge gained from didactic coursework.

THE AGING NETWORK

Counselors working with older persons who are preparing to retire or who have retired should have information about the various services in the community available to older persons. This information will be useful to counselors as well as to their older clients. Probably the best source for such information is the area agency on aging, through which federal and state funds are channeled for services for older persons in local communities.

Table 4 Topics Related to Aging and Counseling for Which Respondents Reported Information Needs

Category	Topic	Rank within category
Counseling strategies and techniques	Applied counseling technique with older persons	1
	Managing/treating depression in older persons	1
	Increasing older clients' motivation for change	1
	Counseling families of older persons	1
	Group counseling techniques	2
	Support groups for older persons	3
	Activity therapies	4
	Use of reminiscence of gerocounseling	4
	Strategies for supportive counseling	5
	New advances in counseling older clients	5
	Instilling hope in older persons	5
Special issues and populations	Counseling older persons who want to die	1
	Helping clients cope with loss	2
	Sexual counseling techniques	3
	Helping clients adjust to role changes with advancing age	4
	Helping older persons adjust to physical decline	4
	Preparing clients and their families for nursing home placement	4
	Helping aging parents adjust to changing parent–child relationships	4
	Counseling terminally ill clients	4
	Ethics in gerontological counseling and research	5
Psychological aspects of aging	General: psychological aspects of aging	1
	Psychological aspects of death and dying	2
	Developmental changes in psychotic patients with advancing age	2
	Common concerns of the older persons	3
	Alzheimer's disease	4
	Aging and work force participation	4
	Older person in the criminal system	5
Consultation programming	Strategies for structuring older persons' physical/social environments	1
	Community resources for older persons	2

Table 4   Topics Related to Aging and Counseling for Which Respondents Reported Information Needs (*Continued*)

Category	Topic	Rank within category
	Establishing prevention programs for older persons	3
	Program development/implementation maintenance procedures	4
	Support/consultation models for working with nursing home staff	4
	Networking techniques	5
Assessment	Assessment techniques with older persons	1
	Neuropsychological assessment	1
	Assessing geriatric depression	2

Each agency on aging is part of an organization of national and state groups that is identified as the Aging Network. At the top of the pyramid is the United States Congress, which appropriates funds through the Older Americans Act. Also in Washington, D.C., are the Department of Health and Human Services, with its Office of Human Development Services and the Administration on Aging. These offices are responsible for budgets and programs for services for older persons on a national basis (12).

The 10 regional offices of the Administration on Aging are assigned a coordinating responsibility for the appropriate state plans which apportion aging programs and services. There are 56 state units on aging, one for each of the 50 states plus U.S. territories. Each state unit on aging designates the various area agencies on aging within the state and approves their plans; there are approximately 600 area agencies on aging in the United States. The state units on aging have major planning and development functions, plus preparation of the State Plan on Aging and allocation of available funds. The area agencies on aging provide an essential link between the governments which provide the funds and the older citizens for whom they are intended.

Major duties of an area agency on aging are to select the service providers who contract with the agency for the various services available to older citizens and to award the necessary support funds. Services include senior centers which oversee and coordinate such activities as telephone reassurance, friendly visitors, legal aid, health programs, and social and information programs, together with the many volunteers who help these services to function.

Another major duty is to provide a nutrition program for older persons that includes home-delivered meals and congregate meal sites. The first program provides delivery of one meal a day, 5 days a week, to the homes of frail older persons. The second program combines serving nutritious meals in a group setting with a social stimulation for participants.

Some area agencies also provide information regarding services within their geographical areas by means of computers and direct-dial telephones to assist older persons and their families.

IMPLICATIONS FOR COUNSELORS

Counseling has been described as a special type of helping relationship that includes both preventive and remedial goals. An overall goal is to facilitate the independence and full functioning of each person. To achieve the many possible goals in working with older persons, a variety of roles can be taken. To perform effectively in these roles, counselors must be aware of their own attitudes and biases and how these might affect their work with older clients.

Preparation of gerontological counselors involves learning both generic and specialized skills. Knowing counseling needs of older persons and sharpening counseling techniques for use with older persons are essential. The area of retirement and preretirement counseling should be especially targeted, according to results of studies cited above. Opportunities for supervised practice and feedback from faculty and on-site supervisors will help to ensure the training of skilled clinicians to meet the mental health and developmental needs of a broad spectrum of older persons.

Regardless of the setting in which counselors find themselves, irrespective of the goals for clients in that setting or the roles in which the counselors function, one final component is necessary to ensure continued, effective services. Counselors must make themselves aware of and participate in opportunities for continuing professional education. The needs of older persons are varied and changing, as is the knowledge base in counseling. Counselors must challenge themselves to continue professional growth if they are to help older persons maximize their potential for positive mental health.

GROUP ACTIVITIES

Divide participants into groups of three to five persons. Ask each group to review the list of goals and roles for counselors shown in Tables 1–4. Have each group choose one goal and discuss the impact of this goal in each of the five life arenas. Then, choose one role and discuss the impact of this role in each of the five life arenas. Ask the group to answer each of the following:

1 What is the difference in impact when discussing goals versus roles?
2 What are the implications of this difference for counseling services and counselor training?

Discuss reactions of the small groups in the full group at the end of the session.

REFERENCES

  1 Havighurst, R. J. (1972). *Developmental tasks and education.* New York: McKay.
  2 Sherman, E. (1981). *Counseling the aging: An integrative approach.* New York: Free Press.
  3 Johnson, R. P., & Riker, H. C. (1982). Counselors' goals and roles in assisting older persons. *American Mental Health Counselors Association Journal, 4*(1), 30–40.
  4 Maslow, A. H. (1970). *Motivation and personality.* New York: Harper.
  5 Combs, A. W. (Ed.). (1962). *Perceiving, behaving, becoming.* Washington, DC: Association for Supervision and Curriculum Development, National Education Association.
  6 Bonner, H. (1967). The proactive personality. In J. F. T. Bugertol (Ed.), *Challenges of humanistic psychology* (pp. 61–66). New York: McGraw-Hill.
  7 Rogers, C. (1961). *On becoming a person.* Boston: Houghton Mifflin.
  8 Blake, R. (1978). *Appropriateness of various counselor roles and activities.* Unpublished manuscript.
  9 Robison, F. F., Comas, R., Blaas, C., Kirk, W., & Freeman, S. (1985, March). *Gerontological counselors in the workplace: Description of professional backgrounds, activities, and information needs.* Paper presented to the meeting of the American Association for Counseling and Development, Los Angeles, CA.
 10 Myers, J. E., & Blake, R. (1986). Professional preparation of gerontological counselors. *Association for Counselor Education and Supervision Journal, 26*(2), 137–145.
 11 Myers, J. E. (1988). *Infusing gerontological counseling into counselor preparation: Curriculum guide.* Alexandria, VA: American Association for Counseling and Development.
 12 Oberle, J. (1981). The aging network. In J. E. Myers, P. Finnerty-Reid, & C. Graves (Eds.), *Counseling older persons* (Vol. 1, pp. 11–18). Alexandria, VA: American Association for Counseling and Development.

Chapter Four

Life Planning

Planning for one's life after retirement begins well before that event—at least 10 years for some of the anticipated changes in life style, many years for others. For example, financial planning should be considered shortly after taking one's very first job. Planning for leisure-time interests other than employment should be incorporated into years at college, for those who attend college, or into the early years of employment. Planning really goes on throughout the process of living. It is just as vital to the person considering retirement as it is to the younger person deciding on job alternatives for the first time.

The purpose of Chapter 2 was to show that individuals, particularly older individuals, must be encouraged to recognize that *all* periods of their lives are important—the early, the middle, and the later. It is the third, or later, period that has been misunderstood and neglected. The purpose of this chapter is to point out some of the many factors that are essential for individuals in planning more effectively for the later period of their lives.

Basic issues shall be discussed that bear directly on planning for one's future. These issues include clarifying one's self-concept, examining one's present value system, identifying one's needs in terms of life satisfaction, and learning to appreciate oneself. Having addressed these issues, individuals must take the important action steps of setting personal goals, identifying the developmental tasks to be accomplished during their present life stage, and making decisions that will result in the achievement of their goals. A wellness lifestyle that includes goals for healthy living is described. Finally, the implications for counselors of the elements involved in retirement planning, together with group activities intended to alert participants to the importance of these various elements, are presented.

In the minds of many people retirement is not associated with planning. In fact, it has been said that people frequently spend more time in planning for their summer vacation than for their retirement. For younger and older people alike the procedures of planning have many common elements, such as examining personal values, setting personal goals, considering alternative courses of action for each of those goals, solving problems, and making decisions.

For their own planning purposes, older persons might find it useful to review studies describing the experiences of other older persons, and the typical life changes that have been reported by others (1). The first change, perhaps, is in the sense of time. Those in the age range of 18 to 42 refer to time in terms of their date of birth. For this age group, time is an unlimited commodity for use in exploring activities in the present and planning those in the future. Individuals in the general age group of 55–75 and onward, tend to think of the future in terms of time left to live. During this later period of life, time seems more limited and there is a sense of urgency to complete certain life tasks. Activities include self-examination and a tendency to become more introspective and contemplative.

During the first half of their lives, men and women concentrate on success in their job, giving some of their attention to a variety of civic and social activities. They tend to gain competence and self-confidence, together with a sense of autonomy. Beginning in midlife and extending into later age, men become more supportive of others and more concerned about relationships. During this period more women take jobs and tend to become more aggressive, self-confident, and independent. Increasingly, women are entering the labor market at earlier ages, and face the challenge of balancing family and work roles.

In their late 40s and early 50s, both men and women often change their attitudes toward life planning. Men may look forward to a more relaxed lifestyle, preferring the environment of home. Women, on the other hand, may prefer a more active way of living, away from the home. Married couples are likely to experience a strong divergence of interests and preferences, sometimes going in opposite directions. When understood, this divergence can be accommodated by both parties. Otherwise, long-standing relationships can be strained and broken.

A second change is a growing awareness of one's life cycle, which encourages a review of one's past life. Other changes include the emergence of a sense of life fulfillment, a feeling that one has done his or her best. At the same time, older persons desire and discover that they have a capacity for continued growth.

For older people, in particular, the subject of planning should include self-identity and important elements in their social and physical environments. These elements encompass health, both physical and mental; relationships with others; time, especially the use of it; a place to live; a new lifestyle; and financing this changed lifestyle.

THE SEARCH FOR SELF

At various stages throughout life, individuals find themselves asking the philosophical question "Who am I?" The answer to this question is, basically, "I am, in part, what I believe others who know me think I am." Ideas about oneself come from interaction with others in the person's environment. The physical image that a person holds of him- or herself also influences ideas about self.

There are three major elements of the self: the self-concept, the self-ideal, and self-esteem (2). The self-concept is the person's perception of what he or she is like. The self-ideal is a result of personal standards gained from various role models and experiences. Self-esteem is the person's evaluation of how well the self-concept compares with the self-ideal. How well the person fulfills various social roles can significantly influence this evaluation. Therefore, the extent to which older persons reduce their social roles can reduce their self-esteem. The relationship between active participation in community life and self-esteem should be apparent.

Another important element in the development of the self-concept is that it occurs gradually over the life span of the person. Erikson emphasized this fact in his description of the eight stages of humans (3). His proposition was that each stage involves alternatives and an individual's selection of an alternative strongly affects each later stage. The first five stages occur in childhood and adolescence (as listed in Chapter 2). The sixth stage embraces early adulthood and involves the choice of intimacy versus isolation. The seventh stage occurs in middle adulthood and the alternatives are generativity versus stagnation. The eighth stage covers a period called "maturity" or later adulthood, and the choice lies between ego integrity versus despair.

Ego integrity is a quality involving order and meaning; it is an acceptance of one's life as it has been lived. This quality produces a sense of satisfaction with one's particular lifestyle, to the extent that the approach of death can be viewed with a certain amount of composure. Ego integrity brings a feeling of trust in the outcomes of one's life. It serves as an effective balance to the potential for despair.

Peck (4) has interpreted Erikson's eighth stage of life as involving three major tasks to be accomplished by the older person. The first is for individuals moving into retirement to release their work as a principal life role and to establish different activities as the primary sources of personal satisfaction and sense of worth. This task can be very difficult for persons who have focused on the job for 30 years or more and have built their value system around this job.

The second task is for older persons to review their value system and their emphasis on physical ability. Since muscle strength and body functions are reduced and less efficient as persons grow older, there is a need for acceptance of these limitations and discomforts and a substitution of intellectual and social abilities to give personal rewards and feelings of self-effectiveness. More attention to personal relationships and continued learning are positive actions in the achievement of this task. Maintaining a reasonable physical exercise program, when feasible, will be helpful.

The third task involves recognition of the inevitability of one's personal death. An additional part of this task is to adopt attitudes and a lifestyle that emphasize activities, the results of which extend beyond one's death. Such activities might include financial or personal assistance to relatives, friends, or appropriate projects in the community. A further part of this task is for older persons to consider themselves as belonging to a universality that extends from the past, through the present, and into the future. Death then becomes another developmental stage. Religion provides contact with at least part of this concept. Essential is seeing the self as one of an infinite number of elements in a totality of universal existence. The point is that the importance of self lies in its being part of an immense wholeness.

This eighth stage of life, ego integrity, represents the achievement of a maturation process whereby older persons see themselves more completely as human beings. Their lives take on a richer, fuller meaning and their future is brighter because of the possibility of their merging with infinity. A significant part of this total process is the gradual overhaul of their value system.

EXAMINING ONE'S VALUE SYSTEM

A value is the quality of an idea or thing that makes it desirable or useful. Individuals' values are ordered into a system arranged in priorities as guides to their thinking and actions. Values are generally learned out of experiences in the family, the school, the community, and the workplace.

According to a study by Rokeach (5), values may be classified as "instrumental" or "terminal." Instrumental values describe desirable ways of behaving; terminal or outcome values indicate desirable goals for action. There is considerable similarity between values held by men and women. As people grow older, they tend to give greater emphasis to outcome values (6). Aging often produces value changes in the direction of adaptation.

Lowenthal, Thurber, and Chiriboga (7) studied 216 middle-class men and women representing four pretransitional stages of life: high school, newlywed, middle-aged, and preretirement. In terms of stated values, their responses to questions fell into seven major categories: personal achievement, marriage and family, humanitarian–moral concerns, coping with the requirements of living, happiness, religious life, and legacy (personal impact on future generations). The older groups tended to emphasize modest goals and coping with the requirements of living.

Those in the preretirement stage indicated a preference for humanitarian and moral purposes. The men stressed their contributions in the form of a legacy while the women focused on religious life. The people in this stage seemed to communicate a "certain transcendence of self and family" (7, p. 180) and to broaden their interests to include a greater variety of persons. Women indicated such values as caring, kindness, helpfulness, and usefulness. Men emphasized more material contributions, as well as the pursuit of pleasure and happiness. Men and women alike stressed ease and contentment in this stage. Independence and survival seemed especially important in the later stages of life.

In the preretirement stage, people appeared to have experienced important changes in a majority of their values. These changes seemed to be related to changes occurring in their adult roles and in their sense of social responsibility. According to the Lowenthal et al. study (7, p. 194), the capacity for future changes in values apparently was related to the individual's qualities of self-assurance and acceptance of self.

UNDERSTANDING ONE'S NEEDS

Just as one's value system is an important source of personal motivation, so are human needs. Needs are things that are wanted or regarded as necessary. In an effort to better understand them, Maslow (8) organized human needs according to a hierarchy in which the basic needs must be satisfied before individuals can work toward meeting higher needs.

Maslow described basic needs as physiological needs that are necessary for survival: hunger, in the case of the individual; sex drive in the case of the species. Next up the ladder he listed safety needs, which included security, stability, freedom from fear, and orderliness. The third level of needs concerned relationships to others, bringing feelings of belonging and of love. Without such feelings, individuals may experience loneliness and a sense of separation. Building on such feelings, needs for self-esteem come into focus. At the top of the hierarchy is the need for self-actualization, which is the need for individuals to realize their potentials, to achieve the best they are capable of achieving. This need is similar to Erikson's ego integrity stage. According to these writers, the common quality of healthy, "normal" people is the striving for perfection, as they see perfection.

It was Maslow's belief that self-actualization encompassed as goals the principal virtues in life: truth, honesty, justice, beauty, order, and playfulness, meaning joy, satisfaction, and happiness (9). Moving toward self-actualization, individuals are likely to have in their lives a series of peak experiences. Such experiences are described by Gresham (10) as "surges of energy" and "renewals of power" (p. 2). For him, their result has been a release of energy that has produced the momentum for action in succeeding years, and the power to meet and resolve crises during various life transitions.

Factors Contributing to Life Satisfaction

Several national studies of older people have identified factors that contribute to a sense of life satisfaction. These surveys are the National Survey of the Aged (11), the Retirement History Longitudinal Survey for the Social Security Administration (12), and the Myth and Reality of Aging in America (13). These studies concluded that the factors most vital to the life satisfaction of older people were health, social contacts, education, competence, income, self-concept, trend toward health, and leisure.

A study was made of three different mid-Florida communities in 1986 (14): a large retirement community, a smaller retirement community, and a meal site in a third community. The factors reported by older persons in these communities as most significant to life satisfaction were ranked in the following priority order: self-concept, sense of competence (feeling adequate to cope with situations), physical competence, living with someone, current health, special social contacts, and marital status. These factors can be placed in three general categories: the psychological, the social, and the physical. The ranking of these factors suggests that an older person's evaluation of self is vital to a sense of life satisfaction.

Appreciation of Self

It has been said that individuals are their own best friends and their own worst enemies. Rubin (15) believed that within every person are opposing forces of great power. The first is compassion, which leads to constructive growth and creative actions; the second is self-hate, which leads to self-destruction. He argued for a psychophilosophy of life that will help individuals to enjoy living in the here and now and to face adversity with self-assurance.

Perhaps the first step toward developing a psychophilosophy of life is to examine one's inner self and determine if there are any elements of self-hate. Should any be found, individuals should identify what they are and explore the circumstances surrounding each element. Tracing the cause or causes may be difficult. However, if these causes occurred back in the individual's distant past and can be defined, it may well be that they are no longer relevant. As a result, the causes and the self-hate arising out of them can be discarded and laid to rest. If the individual cannot take this kind of action, seeking the services of a counselor may be the best approach.

Rubin (15, pp. 181–225) described 12 components of a psychophilosophy that are summarized as follows:

1 The first is to believe that "I am because I am." Individuals do not need to justify their existence, based on what they possess or what they achieve. Such individuals believe they are worthy, so they look at themselves with dignity and loyalty. They do not need to conform or to overpower others.

2 The second component is acceptance of oneself, expressed by the words "I am I." Key ideas here are responsibility for oneself, care for oneself, and a healthy appreciation of oneself.

3 The third component is self-care and taking one's needs seriously. This component represents the ideas "I need, I want, I choose." It involves the necessity of differentiating between needs and desires, choosing in ways that contribute to one's well-being and to the process of self-assertion.

4 Fourth is the assertion "I am where I am," which establishes an individual as the center of his or her life and a particular territory as his or her own. One result is a greater sense of security.

5 Fifth is the directive "Be here now," which stresses the point that the past and the future do not exist, only the present. For this reason, individuals should enjoy themselves as they are and where they are. They should live each day as if it were always the first day of their lives, with a sense of newness, mystery, and challenge.

6 The sixth component of Rubin's psychophilosophy points out that life is a process, and the emphasis is on the process, not the product. This component is called "the Process and the Product"; it is intended to help individuals avoid striving for something that they never achieve.

7 The seventh component, called "I always do my best," stresses self-acceptance, that is, what individuals accomplish at any given time may not be their best effort, but it was the best they were capable of at that time.

8 The eighth component conveys the idea that human beings are complex and at times inconsistent. This means that individuals do not always operate in rational ways or make reasonable decisions.

9 The ninth, an important component for individuals, is the right to say "no." This right is a self-preserving mechanism that emphasizes value systems and avoids feelings of self-hate.

10 The 10th component calls attention to the difference between participation and performance. The former refers to complete involvement in and full contribution to physical, intellectual, and emotional activities. The latter produces self-consciousness, self-judgment, and fear of criticism from other people. The former is self-enhancing and rewarding; the latter is self-defeating.

11   The 11th component involves individuals' feelings about death; it is called "the Right to Die and the Right to Live." The attitude expressed by the Right to Die can free individuals from the fear of death and strengthen their ability to live. On the other hand, the assertion of the Right to Live conveys to individuals the belief that as long as they are alive, they will make the most of living. The Right to Die helps to reduce the guilt associated with dying and the sense of failing to discharge one's responsibilities.

12   The 12th, and last, component is acceptance of the saying "Life is tough." Individuals have great assets to use in meeting the challenges of living. Yet, they are often unprepared to face life's problems; they struggle to survive and to enjoy living. Knowing that life is tough and accepting that fact makes living a little easier; this knowledge helps individuals to value more what they can accomplish. The feeling of deep sympathy, or compassion, for oneself and for others helps to make life easier and more worthwhile.

Rubin's psychophilosophy and its components underscore the importance of living fully today and, in the process, realizing one's potentials. Most human beings are engaged in a never-ending effort to match their values and behaviors in order to achieve ego integrity, to enjoy themselves and the world about them. Understanding and respecting oneself is an indispensable first step. A positive approach to living is a second.

SETTING GOALS

Rubin's (15) psychophilosophy provides a constructive way to look at oneself and set goals for oneself. These goals represent desired results or achievements toward which personal efforts can be directed. Some older persons are likely to think that goal setting is for younger people. Yet goals give vital direction and meaning to the process of living at any age; without them, individuals may flounder, regardless of age.

One useful approach to the topic of goals for living is for persons to look at their present lives and identify existing problem areas that need attention. When these problems are defined, individuals can turn them around and make their solutions the goals to be achieved. For example, an older person may be concerned about poor relationships with his or her married children and their families. The goal becomes improving relationships with family members.

In general terms, important goals to be considered by persons over 55 years of age might be described as follows:

Adopting a New Life Style.   Leaving one's full-time job usually means a change in one's daily routine, leaving fellow workers and familiar work settings, and developing new procedures for living. This process is commonly called retirement, which many see as an ending, a withdrawal, and a settling back, but which, in actuality, just means *change,* from one particular lifestyle to another. To the extent that this period of time represents to older persons a new beginning they may react with enthusiasm and may look for new opportunities for living. Some additional goals should give substance to a new lifestyle.

Maintaining or Developing Physical and Mental Health. According to recent studies, decline in physical health may be attributed less to aging and more to disuse of muscles and body functions (16). This decline is much more reversible than was once believed. Intellectual abilities of older adults apparently do not decline as much as become obsolete (17). The important point to remember is that the knowledge store of some older persons can become obsolescent or obsolete and need replenishing and updating, usually through additional education and training.

Understanding the Aging Process. Aging is a process of change and adapting to change; it is a process of growing and developing throughout the life cycle. Aging should be thought of not only in physical terms, but also in intellectual, emotional, and spiritual terms.

Aging involves both happiness and sorrow. Older persons suffer losses of family members and friends. They gain the richness of experience, maturity, and a sense of completeness. But such results do not just happen; they require planning, willpower, and rigorous development of one's abilities.

The life view of individuals is important: to keep looking forward and regard changes as situations to be overcome or as challenges to be met. The causes for aging are not really known. However, a positive attitude toward life is one of the major ingredients for successful aging.

Strengthening Family Relationships. The family often provides a sense of security, a feeling of belonging, and a source of affection and love. When older persons leave full-time employment, they can expect to be at home during more hours of a day. This change is likely to bring about an altering of relationships with the spouse who may or may not be at home. Differences that have existed for a long time may be magnified; sometimes, there is a need for the couple to get reacquainted with each other and their changing roles in the family. This change in lifestyle may enable the couple to establish new relationships and renew their love for each other.

Changes in relationships with adult children and their families also occur. The older couple no longer has the parent role in the family. This role shifts to that of senior family member, minus the authority and responsibility of the parent. In fact, the adult children gradually assume responsibility for the well-being of their parents and, in this sense at least, take on the parent role of the original family. This shift in family roles must be recognized by all family members, because it causes a change in relationships. As this change is understood, family relations can be accepted and strengthened.

Strengthening Spiritual Life. Throughout their lives, individuals are engaged in establishing relationships: first, with others in their environment; second, with their own inner selves; and third, with some higher power representing the Infinite. In each case, individuals are asking the same question: "Who am I?" Other questions are raised, often as persons grow older: "Why am I here?" "What is the meaning of my life?" "Where am I going?"

Answers to these questions may be sought in one's established religion and/or in study of life philosophies. Religious groups can offer reassuring answers to these questions. Various schools of life philosophies can do so also. Required of individuals, in either case, is the development of a personal trust and faith, a strengthening of their spiritual life arena that provides a sense of connection with an infinite power and a firmer assurance of life's meaning.

Strengthening Self-Concept. As already indicted, self-concept is the person's perception of what he or she is like. This perception is vital to self-image and self-esteem. If positive, it enables persons to move toward realizing their potential. If negative, it can inhibit personal growth. Self-concept reflects the impact of experiences; it also indicates the strength of persons' beliefs about themselves.

Including the strengthening of self-concept as a goal for later life pinpoints the importance of maintaining a positive perception of self and continuing to build a solid sense of self-worth. All of the goals listed above are intended to produce feelings of self-satisfaction in older persons and to counteract negative feelings of self that sometimes can develop.

Bengston (18) has described a "social breakdown syndrome: a vicious cycle of increasing incompetence" (p. 47). The elements of this cycle are a susceptibility to psychological breakdown, social labeling as incompetent, induction into a sick or dependent role, and self-identification as sick or inadequate. This downward spiral of negative conditions is often hard to break out of, and the eventual result is depression, which is a very common problem, especially among older persons.

To counter this situation, Bengston suggested a program for increasing the older person's sense of competence. This program includes building self-confidence and self-reliance, identifying oneself as able, fostering coping skills, and strengthening the self-view as an effective person. It is quite possible that an older person should seek the aid of a professional counselor in rebuilding a positive self-concept. Better still, actively pursuing the life goals already listed often can prevent negative views of oneself from developing.

An additional goal, enjoying living, reinforces and builds on the goal of strengthening the self-concept. The later phase of life opens up opportunities for free time, leisure activities, and the development of latent skills. However, several problems may be encountered. A major one is the inability of some persons to enjoy living. They have become conditioned to work at a job, to follow a carefully constructed schedule, and to measure accomplishments on the basis of material rewards, in the form of salary increases and promotions.

Enjoyment of living for its own sake implies a variety of activities, a flexible schedule, and rewards in the form of inner joy.

Bloomfield and Kory (19) defined inner joy as involving self-confidence, inner harmony, and a sense of vitality. "Inner joy is a state of being, not a result of doing" (p. 13). Avoidance of a sense of joy for its own sake is a behavior long supported by the American society and the educational system. Depending on the viewpoint of the particular persons, joy or pleasure for no other purpose has been regarded as a waste of time, an activity without rewards, or even sinful. Although this viewpoint seems to be changing, it is still common among many of today's older persons. In these cases, individuals should find it helpful to look at their own well-being as the most important objective in their lives and to adopt behaviors that will support this objective. Lifelong learning programs may also be used by older persons to focus attention on enjoyment of present living.

Progress toward these goals may be best achieved by identifying developmental tasks that, when completed, enable individuals to reach their goals. Havighurst described these tasks as those necessary for individuals' healthy and satisfactory growth in their particular environment (20). Such tasks should support the growth patterns of older persons.

DEVELOPMENTAL TASKS

Adopting the point of view that the human life span is made up of a series of developmental stages, older persons will understand that each stage includes a series of developmental tasks. Those tasks must be accomplished successfully before individuals can move to the next life stage. In Chapter 2, these stages were described as occurring one after the other from birth to death, each requiring a time span of some 7–8 years, with transition periods between them of 2–3 years each.

For the purposes of life planning, older persons should review the various life stages and their accompanying developmental tasks to get a fuller understanding of the life span as a totality. A closer study might then be made of the various tasks associated with the life stages beginning with age 56 and continuing through age 104. Two points will be discovered as such a study is made: (a) Life changes are frequent at all ages and adaptation to change is a continuing task, and (b) some tasks are repeated during the various life stages, in the earlier, middle, and later years of life. Stated another way, some tasks are important for persons of *various* ages to consider and accomplish. Successful resolution or achievement of a task at one life stage is not an end in itself, but a means to continued successful coping with similar, perhaps identical, tasks in later years. Table 1 represents one way to organize developmental tasks as guides for action by persons in or near the later period of their lives. These tasks have been identified on the basis of three assumptions: (a) Life tasks

Table 1   Developmental Tasks of Later Life by Life Arenas

Life arena

The 50s—Questioning work and leisure values, ages 56-64

Career
1. Redefining the work role
2. Leaving full-time job
3. Selecting part-time job
4. Adjusting to lifestyle changes
5. Volunteering to serve others
6. Reassesing financial status

Family
1. Renewing/strengthening relations with spouse
2. Accepting losses in family
3. Assisting aging parents
4. Relating to married children
5. Adjusting to grandparenting roles and grandchildren

Leisure
1. Achieving a new definition of leisure
2. Managing leisure time and activities
3. Assessing physical and mental health

Leisure (*Cont.*):
4. Adjusting exercise and nutrition programs

Intimacy
1. Maintaining/strengthening existing relationships
2. Building new friendships
3. Adjusting to single status
4. Extending capacity to share oneself with others

Inner life
1. Becoming reacquainted with self
2. Building understanding of external Life Force
3. Adjusting to physical and mental health changes
4. Managing stress
5. Reviewing one's life history
6. Striving for integrity

The 60s—Redefining the busyness ethic, ages 65-74

Career
1. Redefining life and work roles
2. Leaving full-time job
3. Considering part-time job
4. Participating in job retraining program
5. Searching for community involvment
6. Reviewing financial status
7. Engaging in volunteer activities

Family
1. Reviewing relations with spouse/adult children
2. Reevaluating roles within the family
3. Accepting losses of family members and friends
4. Deciding on place to live
5. Reassesing personal expectations of family members and friends
6. Strengthening personal relationships

Leisure
1. Redefining leisure roles
2. Managing leisure time and activities
3. Assessing physical and mental health

Leisure (*Cont.*):
4. Adjusting exercise and nutrition programs
5. Reviewing/limiting use of medical drugs

Intimacy
1. Strengthening existing relationships
2. Building new friendships
3. Adjusting to single status
4. Extending capacity to share oneself with others

Inner life
1. Searching for life's meanings
2. Evaluating personal strengths and weaknesses
3. Strengthening relations with external Life Force
4. Reviewing personal attitudes toward death
5. Managing stress
6. Reviewing one's life history
7. Striving for integrity

Table 1 Developmental Tasks of Later Life by Life Arenas (*Continued*)

Life arena

The 70s—Reviewing the past, planning the future, ages 75–84

Career
1. Releasing work as a principal life role
2. Limiting work schedules
3. Curtailing job involvement
4. Reviewing financial status

Family
1. Evaluating and strengthening family relationships
2. Reviewing living arrangements
3. Expanding friendship circle
4. Affiliating with own age groups
5. Investing in grandparenthood
6. Reviewing transportation resources

Leisure
1. Strengthening leisure self-concept
2. Reassessing physical/mental health
3. Adjusting exercise and nutrition programs
4. Developing new skills
5. Exploring opportunities for creativity

Intimacy
1. Maintaining sexual identity
2. Adjusting attitudes toward sexuality
3. Developing and sharing intellectual interests
4. Cultivating caring feelings toward others
5. Improving ability to communicate with others

Inner life
1. Building on life history's successes
2. Strengthening life's meanings
3. Clarifying relationship with external Life Force
4. Becoming more satisfied with self
5. Recreating one's self-image in terms of current life circumstances
6. Managing stress
7. Striving for integrity

The 80s—Strengthening one's sense of self and of personal power, ages 85–94

Career
1. Evaluating work activities
2. Limiting work commitments
3. Reviewing use of time
4. Examining financial status

Family
1. Clarifying personal roles in family
2. Providing financial or personal assistance to family members
3. Strengthening friendship circles
4. Creating substitute family
5. Enjoying grandparenthood status

Leisure
1. Maintaining exercise and nutrition programs
2. Selecting areas for new learning experiences

Leisure (*Cont.*):
3. taking time for reflection
4. Expanding creative activities

Intimacy
1. Maintaining/enhancing relationships with others
2. Participating with social support groups
3. Assessing emotional maturity
4. Coping with physical changes
5. Becoming more satisfied with self

Inner life
1. Clarifying life's meanings
2. Clarifying concepts of death and right to die
3. Developing inner peace
4. Achieving integrity

Table 1   Developmental Tasks of Later Life by Life Arenas (*Continued*)

Life arena	
The 90s — Building spiritual wholeness, ages 95–104	
Career	Intimacy
1. Combining work and leisure activities	1. Maintaining/enhancing relationships with others
2. Emphasizing hobby interests	2. Maintaining emotional satisfaction
3. Maintaining information on career areas of interest	3. Coping with physical changes
Family	Inner life
1. Enhancing family relationships	1. Achieving sense of spiritual wholeness
2. Enjoying family roles	2. Strengthening relationships with and relying on external Life Force
3. Joining with surrogate family units	3. Maintaining/enjoying integrity
Leisure	
1. Managing time and resources	
2. Appreciating leisure activities as substitutes for work	

should be positive, (b) participation in activities represents a healthy approach to growing older, and (c) in our lives there tends to be an evolution from a concern about relationships to other persons to a concern about relationships to oneself and one's God. Some of the tasks listed for a particular time period may not be applicable to all older persons, because they differ in their stages of development. For this reason, older persons should consider the tasks included in their age group in Table 1 in terms of their own needs, selecting those tasks that apply to their particular stage of development, their life arenas, and their life enhancement.

The developmental tasks included in the time span from age 56 to age 104 all concern reacting to change and building positive life concepts. The 50s are often a time for questioning work and leisure values and for redefining personal roles in the various life arenas. There is renewed emphasis on relationships with others and becoming reacquainted with oneself.

The 60s may involve a careful look at one's life habits, to replacing busyness for its own sake with personal involvement in helping others, developing one's own capacities, and searching for new life meanings.

The 70s continue a review of the past in terms of planning for the future. This is a period when leisure activities become more important than work, family and friendship relationships grow in significance, and the search for life's meaning intensifies. The 80s provide opportunities for aging persons to strengthen their sense of self and their feelings of personal power. These opportunities may be found through continuing to develop family and friendship circles, expanding creative activities, coping with physical changes, taking more time for reflection, and achieving inner peace.

The 90s are a period for individuals to build their sense of spiritual wholeness. This is a time when the problems of the past become inconsequential, when present relationships and activities are to be enjoyed for themselves, and when the uncertainties of the future can be faced with composure. For the 90s and beyond individuals may focus on enjoying their lives through appreciating the events of each day and the people who enter into those days.

MAKING DECISIONS

Making decisions about a plan of action for personal growth and development are among the most important decisions individuals will make, especially for those over 50. The reasons are threefold. First, these decisions will establish patterns of living for the later part of life and govern the directions for thinking and action during that time. Second, thee decisions will heavily influence, if not determine, the quality and vitality of life to be lived by older persons who would prefer to involved in planning their future; otherwise, their lives are likely to be aimless and they may drift without direction. Third, there are few guidelines to use as models, principally because in the past people generally did not live as long as they do now and life after retirement was generally regarded as limited in value and potential. That situation is changing dramatically as people find they are living as many years after full-time employment as during full-time employment.

Another factor enters into the issue of decision making. Many persons, younger as well as older, have little practical experience in making decisions affecting their living and well-being. During most of their lives, decisions have been made for them, at home, during school years, and at work. When there is no one else to make decisions for them people may panic, hastily choosing a course of action that meets neither their honest preferences nor their best interests. Gelatt's (21) concept of decision making is the basis for the following discussion.

The process of decision making starts with selection of a goal or objective that represents the solution of a problem. The individual quickly becomes aware that information is needed and that there are several possible ways to approach the goal. Accordingly, information is collected and possible alternative actions are listed, preferably in writing. Each alternative is evaluated in terms of its positive and negative consequences.

At this point, the individual's value system comes into play and consideration is given to the desirability of the possible outcomes. When the alternative emerges with the most desirable outcome, from the individual's point of view, the decision is made to adopt that particular course of action.

There are several difficulties faced in this process. The first is friends or relatives who are glad to offer their advice. This advice is often taken by the persons who place great value on the opinion of others and who do not want to make their own decisions. The second difficulty is that important personal decisions tend to be complex and the situation is likely to be confusing, if not overwhelming. An approach to this difficulty is to break down the goal into component parts that can be managed. The third difficulty is that the individual may lack the criteria for determining if an alternative is positive or negative. Possible criteria for judging an alternative to be positive are that it makes the person feel good, is compatible with his or her general attitudes toward life, and has useful, practical results. To determine that an alternative is negative, the person would note that it makes him or her feel bad, it is not really compatible with his or her attitudes toward life, and its results may be detrimental. An additional difficulty is that in most situations the best alternative is neither all good nor all bad, but mixed. The choice involves shades of gray.

This decision-making process requires individuals to set aside adequate time for selecting a goal, considering possible alternative courses of action necessary to reach it, the desirability of their outcomes, and the selection of one over the others. Additional factors are the adequacy of information that relates to the goal and the individual's confidence in his or her ability to define and think through possible courses of action and choose one as preferable. Experience is important to this process, as is recognition that trial and error are involved. It should be understood that some decisions may be tentative and that further investigation might bring about a change. One very important area of decision making is developing one's lifestyle, particularly a wellness lifestyle.

WELLNESS LIFESTYLE

Wellness is a way of looking at one's health that includes physical, mental, emotional, and spiritual components. It starts with an individual's view of self as a growing, changing person. It moves in positive ways toward understanding and realizing one's potentials. Wellness really means that persons are basically responsible for their own health.

The wellness model begins with the premise that the individual is well and that the objective is for the person to stay that way. In short, persons maintain responsibility for their own state of health and select those activities that will foster a continued state of health. The important factor is recognizing those activities that promote health as well as those that do not. In this sense, individuals become their own physicians; they are less reliant on others. In contemporary America, adults have tended to regard their health as the particular province of medical personnel, forgetting that the primary responsibility remains their own.

The objectives of wellness are happiness, inner joy, and acceptance of self and others. The four major elements of wellness are self-responsibility, stress management, adequate nutrition, and physical fitness (22).

Self-Responsibility

Most important to wellness is the element of self-responsibility. The key idea here is that adults are accountable for themselves and their health. Perhaps the greatest reason for lack of health is neglect of oneself. Some people may prefer to be sick because sickness gives them more attention by others.

Each person benefits from a positive approach to life, from a point of view that he or she is basically the cause for a condition of wellness. This approach grows out of a sense of purpose for living; this purpose is simply happiness, whatever that means to the particular person. Self-responsibility also alerts the person when the need arises to call on medical specialists for assistance.

Stress Management

Selye has defined stress as a "nonspecific response of the body to any demand made upon it" (23, p. 14). Stress can be positive or negative. Everyone needs stress in some situations; it provides energy and motivation in coping with important events. But stress can be negative. It can turn into distress and drain a person's energy; it can wear down resistance to depression or illness, which is often stress related.

Stress is frequently created by individuals' own perceptions of events and people around them. Tubering (24) lists four sets of skills used in managing stress. The first comprises personal management skills such as determining one's values, developing an action plan, using time carefully, and estimating time required to perform a task. The second set includes relationship skills, which involve an individual's changing his or her ways in interacting with other people. The third set comprises outlook skills to provide new ways of looking at life experiences. And the fourth set includes physical stamina skills, which provide personal strength to meet the particular situations perceived as stressful.

The significant point about the management of stress is managing oneself. Building self-confidence provides the core of support for managing oneself.

Nutrition and physical fitness, important elements of wellness, are discussed in Chapter 5.

IMPLICATIONS FOR COUNSELORS

In order to be helpful to older persons who are planning for the rest of their lives, primarily in retirement, counselors ought to have experienced planning in their own lives. Particularly, counselors need to be familiar with developmental theories and their emphasis on life stages and on developmental tasks associated with each stage.

Of major importance is counselor knowledge of a psychophilosophy as espoused by Rubin (15) and of wellness programs with their various positive elements (16). If aging is to be viewed as a growth process, the ultimate goal is the flowering and maturing of the self. That objective may best be realized when individuals see the importance of enjoying living in the here and now, day by day. Enjoyment includes appreciation of self, living fully, and experiencing an inner happiness that is reflected outwardly toward family, friends, and associates. Aging, then, is a continuing, positive aspect of life and one to be cultivated all along the life span.

Planning for one's life should be seen as an activity which is often repeated during the lifespan, by both younger and older persons. Advance and continued planning are especially important to those who are, or soon will be, in retirement. This planning must include financial security, leisure interests, family relationships, and friendship groups. Good planning requires setting goals, solving problems, and reaching decisions.

In addition to experience with the processes of planning and the knowledge relevant to the needs and interests of persons in retirement, counselors must recognize that all of human life has purpose and all human beings have potential. This is to say that counselors must come to appreciate aging and recognize the particular virtues associated with growing older. Especially, they must overcome their socially induced prejudices against aging and older people.

In helping older persons, counselors should remember that each one has had a variety of life experiences and yet may not have seen the values of personal goals to give direction and purpose to later life. Older persons, too, are subject to social prejudices against aging and older people. They differ from younger clients, particularly in the extent of their life experiences. At the same time, they too have important developmental tasks to accomplish, although in a different context.

GROUP ACTIVITIES

I   Plan a fantasy experience. Groups of up to six persons are seated in a circle and asked to imagine that they have retired within the last year. Each group selects two of the following issues and discusses them for a period of about 30 min:

   1   During the next few months, on what activity would I like to spend the greatest part of my time?
   2   If I were to have the opportunity to plan for my retirement all over again, what would I do differently?
   3   What do I enjoy most about my retirement?
   4   Which of the life goals listed in this chapter are the most important, in my opinion?

II Ask group members to read the developmental tasks listed in Table 1 and to select an age group they could identify with during this exercise. Then ask them to respond to the following questions:

1 Of the life arenas listed, which do I regard at this time (selected age group) as the most important for me? Why?
2 Of the developmental tasks listed under the life arena I selected as most important, which do I need to work on first? Why?
3 What developmental tasks would I add to the life arena selected as most important? Why?
4 Do I think the idea of developmental tasks is important? Why?

III In groups of six, ask each group member to respond in turn to the following question:

What are the two or three accomplishments in my life which have meant the most to me?

(Group members may want to jot down ideas on a piece of paper before answering this question for the group.) To which life arena or arenas is each accomplishment most closely linked?

REFERENCES

1 Butler, R. N. (1975). *Why survive: Being old in America.* St. Louis: C. V. Mosby.
2 Sherman, E. (1981). *Integrative counseling.* New York: Free Press.
3 Erikson, E. (1963). *Childhood and society.* New York: Norton.
4 Peck, R. (1968). Psychological developments in the second half of life. In B. L. Neugarten (Ed.), *Middle age and aging* (pp. 88–92). Chicago: University of Chicago Press.
5 Rokeach, M. (1973). *The nature of human value.* New York: Free Press.
6 Neugarten, B. L., Havighurst, R. J., & Tobin, S. J. (1968). Personality and patterns of aging. In B. L. Neugarten (Ed.), *Middle age and aging* (pp. 173–177). Chicago: University of Chicago Press.
7 Lowenthal, M. F., Thurber, M., & Chiriboga, D. (1975). *Four stages of life.* San Francisco: Jossey-Bass.
8 Maslow, A. H. (1970). *Motivation and personality* (2nd ed.). New York: Harper and Row.
9 Schaie, K. W., & Willis, S. L. (1986). *Adult development and aging* (2nd ed.). Boston: Little, Brown.
10 Gresham, P. E. (1980). *With wings as eagles.* Winter Park, FL: Anna.
11 Shanas, E. (1975). *National survey of aged.* Chicago: University of Chicago Press.
12 Social Security Administration. (1981). *Retirement history longitudinal survey. 1975.* Ann Arbor, MI: Inter-University Consortium for Political and Social Research.

13 Harris, L., & Associates. (1975). *The myth and reality of aging in America.* Washington, DC: National Council on the Aging.

14 Doty, L. (1986). *Life satisfaction determinants in older persons.* Unpublished doctoral dissertation, University of Florida, Gainesville.

15 Rubin, T. I. (1975). *Compassion and self-hate: An alternative to despair.* New York: David McKay Company.

16 Dychtwald, K. (1986). *Wellness and health promotion for the elderly.* Rockville, MD: Aspen Systems Corporation.

17 Schaie, K. W. (1975). Age changes in adult intelligence. In D. S. Woodruff & J. E. Berren (Eds.), *Aging* (pp. 111–124). New York: Van Nostrand.

18 Bengston, V. L. (1973). *The social psychology of aging.* Indianapolis: Bobbs Merrill.

19 Bloomfield, H. H., & Kory, R. B. (1980). *Inner joy.* New York: Playboy Paperbacks.

20 Chickering, A. W. (1981). *The modern American college.* San Francisco: Jossey-Bass.

21 Gelatt, H. B. (1962). Decision making: A conceptual frame of reference for counseling. *Journal of Counseling Psychology, 9*(3), 240–245.

22 Ardell, D. B. (1977). *High level wellness.* Emmaus, PA: Rodale Press.

23 Selye, H. (1974). *Stress without distress.* New York: New American Library.

24 Tubering, D. (1981). *Kicking your stress habits.* Duluth, MN: Whole Persons Associates.

Chapter Five

Enjoying Health

One aspect of life planning that has received increasing attention in recent years is health, both physical and emotional. It is clear that each person is unique and this uniqueness increases as persons grow older based on the variety and combination of individual life experiences. One's unique lifestyle includes a variety of habits that carry over into the later years and affect health in tangible as well as intangible ways.

One of the key aspects of adjustment to aging involves maintenance of health. In fact, positive health habits to a great extent will determine the quality of life in one's later years (1). It is entirely possible and highly desirable to maintain good physical and emotional (mental) health in later life (2).

In this chapter, aspects of physical and emotional health, as well as the interrelationship between them, are explored. The discussion of physical health includes an overview of common physiological changes and health concerns associated with aging. Two primary areas that work together to foster good health—exercise and diet—are discussed. Mental health issues included relate to achieving and maintaining a sense of control over one's life and achieving ego integrity. A variety of implications for counselors working with midlife and older individuals are suggested.

PHYSICAL HEALTH

Physical health in later life is related to a number of factors, including heredity, lifestyle, knowledge, and accidents, among others. Achieving and/or maintaining good health is possible at any age. Knowledge of normative aspects of biological aging and common health problems associated with aging can help older persons prepare for and prevent, to a great extent, serious and incapacitating disabilities (1, 3). Developing positive health habits, especially in regard to exercise and nutrition, also is critical in this regard. Each of these issues is discussed below.

Normative Aspects of Physical Change Associated With Aging

Physical change occurs slowly, so slowly that we scarcely are aware of changes until years after they have begun to occur. Physical declines actually begin in the 20s, with changes in visual perceptions and abilities that first become apparent around the age of 40 (3). When any change seems to occur suddenly, immediate medical evaluation and intervention are indicated. Normal change follows a typical, slow, developmental pattern that is evident in all bodily systems. Understanding developmental changes is made more difficult as a result of the extreme variability that exists among people. Each person "ages" at a different rate, biologically, psychologically, and socially. Further, within any given person's life, the rate of change in each of these developmental spheres is not the same (2, 4). The good news is that most age-related changes are not incapacitating.

Some of the more obvious biological changes occur in the skin and hair (2, 3). Loss of elasticity and reduction in the subcutaneous layer of fat beneath the skin create wrinkles. Loss of pigmentation leads to graying of hairs and "spots" on the skin. Vitality is not affected by any of these changes.

Changes occur in each of the sensory organs as well (3). Most common are changes in vision and hearing. Most visual changes lend themselves to correction with adaptive lenses and/or rehabilitative interventions (5). Hearing decrements may be ameliorated with use of a hearing aid, though some types of hearing loss are not correctable in this manner. Surgery for both visual and hearing losses is common and quite successful for most individuals. Since losses in these areas, especially hearing, are commonly associated with aging, older persons may fail to seek medical care when it could be helpful (3, 5, 6).

Changes in taste, touch, and smell become most noticeable in the eighth decade of life and beyond, though again these reflect slow, progressive changes over the life span (3). There is a progressive loss of taste buds and reduction in taste sensitivity so that stronger stimuli (e.g., more spices, more salt) are needed to prevent food from tasting bland. Tactile discrimination declines, so that objects are less easily recognized by touch, especially smooth and/or tiny ones. The sense of smell also decreases, making olfactory identification of substances more difficult for some older persons. Safety also may be affected if older persons are unable to smell spoiled foods, smoke fumes, and so forth.

Progressive changes in the musculoskeletal system after a peak between the ages of 25 and 30 lead to atrophy of muscles and generalized complaints of weakness (3). These changes may be slowed or even reversed through exercise (1). Degenerative joint changes are common, though pain is not always present. Deterioration and brittleness of bones, leading to fractures (especially hip) are more common in older women, especially those whose lifestyle habits have not included exercise or attention to calcium intake (2). Both reaction time and muscular strength decrease so that older persons move more slowly and are capable of less sustained muscular activity (3).

Changes in the nervous system reflect a lifetime of progressive loss of nonregenerating neurons. The result is a slowing in the process of learning new skills, though ability is not affected. There is some research to indicate that fluid intelligence, the ability to learn new things, decreases slightly, but that crystallized intelligence, the stored fund of knowledge a person has, is unaffected by the aging process. The conclusion seems to be that in spite of age-related changes, older persons can continue to learn new knowledge and skills. Adjustments may be necessary in the teaching/learning process to accommodate for decreased reaction times (3, 7).

The respiratory system experiences decrements with aging, most notably a decrease in maximum breathing capacity. The changes occur so slowly over so many years that most older persons do not even notice them; rather, the progressive modification of activities with age serves as a self-regulatory function. Moderation rather than elimination of activities allows most older persons to continue to enjoy the activities and hobbies of their earlier years, while exercise helps to restore and maintain respiratory functioning (1, 3).

Gastrointestinal or digestive changes again reflect a slowing down of system function with age (3). Digestive physicians estimate that a large percentage of the medical complaints of older persons relate to gastrointestinal disorders, with more than half of those complaints being functional and not organic. Poor or ill-fitting dentures, isolation and the lack of persons with whom to share meals, depression, and many other conditions can affect eating habits and contribute to digestive disorders in older persons. It seems that many of the problems associated with aging are felt "at gut level." Public media, especially television commercials for laxatives and antacids, emphasize functional changes in the body system, perhaps encouraging the experiencing of problems that otherwise could be minimized.

Age-related changes in the genitourinary system affect both men and women. After the sixth decade, men are at risk for development of prostate disorders. Urinary incontinence is an increasing problem for aging women, with men affected somewhat as well. Fear of embarrassment or rejection due to incontinence may lead to social withdrawal (3).

Sexual functioning is known *not* to decline significantly with age, except when older persons believe declines should occur (an example of a self-fulfilling prophecy). Older persons maintain both sensual and physical enjoyment, with some modification in sexual routines being a natural outcome of physical changes (8). The major age-related sexual "disorder" is not physical at all. Rather, it is the lack of available partners, especially for older women, that leads to declines in sexual functioning (2, 3). Persons who maintain good health are able to continue satisfying sexual activity into old age (9).

Cardiovascular changes with age also are common, though not inevitable. The major change is reduced circulatory efficiency due to a reduction in cardiac output, defined as the amount of oxygen the blood is able to carry (3). Stroke volume, the amount of blood the heart pumps with each beat, also decreases. Thus, the stage is set for decreased flow of oxygen to all body systems, contributing to a loss of function throughout the body. The aging heart is able to function adequately in nonstressful situations but more slowly with increased age. In the absence of exercise to promote cardiac function, the net result is a variety of physical disabilities. These are discussed briefly below, following by a review of research on prevention and amelioration of age-related, cardiac-system-related disabilities.

Common Health Problems of Older Persons

The three most common causes of deaths in the United States are heart disease, cancer, and stroke, which together account for 65% of deaths in older persons (10). Two of these conditions, heart disease and stroke, are related to dysfunction in the cardiovascular system. These conditions do not appear suddenly, but rather progressively over many years. By the time they are recognized and addressed it may be too late to make major changes. Health factors leading to these three conditions result in progressive physical limitations and disabilities over a number of years (1, 11).

It is estimated that 86% of all older persons have one or more chronic physical conditions that limit their performance of daily living activities (12, 13). Yet, most older persons are as active as they want to be. Only 4–5% of older persons are institutionalized, and only 10–15% are largely homebound because of physical and/or mental infirmities (12). The most commonly reported physical conditions among older persons living in the community (i.e., noninstitutionalized) are arthritis (44%), hypertension (39%), hearing impairment (28%), heart disease (27%), arteriosclerosis (12%), visual impairment (12%), and diabetes (8%) (12).

Most older persons view themselves as being healthy. In fact, 56% of persons over 65 rate their health as excellent or good. Positive health ratings decline with age, especially for those over age 80. Yet 51%—still a majority— of persons over age 80 rate their health as excellent or good. More women and minority individuals tend to rate their health as only fair or poor (14).

Relationship Between Physical Change and Aging

Age-related physical changes are inevitable. However, the physical changes associated with aging do not appear suddenly when one reaches the sixth or seventh decade of life. Rather, these changes are the result of a lifetime of personal health habits and practices (1). Many persons abuse their bodies. The most common abuses include dietary excesses and decrements, being over-weight, smoking, drug use, and sedentary lifestyle. These abuses lead to signif-icant physical limitations for most persons who indulge in them (15).

On the other hand, many researchers have concluded, "Grandmother was right" (16). Persons who engage in positive health habits are found to be healthier and feel better than those who do not (1, 17). The major habits that are recommended include the following: Get 7–8 hr of sleep each night; eat break-fast regularly; avoid eating between meals; remain within a few pounds of your recommended ideal weight; obtain regular, vigorous physical exercise; drink only moderately or not at all; and refrain from smoking.

Clearly, the preponderance of healthy lifestyle recommendations relate to two areas: exercise and diet. Interestingly, these two areas form the core of cardiac rehabilitation, both preventive and remedial. In terms of disability, ex-ercise and diet are the key factors in treating and overcoming the major age-related physical disabilities. In terms of healthy lifestyles, these two factors form the core of good physical functioning over the life span (1, 8, 17).

Exercise

Research on the relationship between exercise and aging has escalated within the last few years. The results are anything but equivocal: Exercise is the only factor that inhibits normal age-related change (1, 3). Further, exercise has been shown to reverse the negative effects of aging in persons in their sixth, seventh, and eight decade, and beyond (17). Many explanations for this situation are possible.

On a simplistic level, oxygen is responsible for efficient operation of all body systems, including the brain. Age-related decrements in the ability of the blood to carry oxygen contribute to declines in all areas of functioning, includ-ing intellectual. Exercise improves cardiac output, that is, the maximum amount of oxygen that the blood is able to carry. Thus, even a small amount of regular exercise improves the functioning of all body systems. Exercise has a direct and positive effect on cardiovascular functioning, regardless of the age at which an exercise program is begun.

All persons should have a physical examination prior to initiating an exercise program. The goal usually is 20–30 min of vigorous physical activity three times per week. This goal need not be met right away. In fact, the major mistake persons make when starting an exercise program is wanting to reach the end of it immediately. Especially for those who have been sedentary for long periods of time, gradual beginnings are necessary. Physician-prescribed exercise programs are among the most successful for older individuals (1).

Virtually any physical exercise that the individual enjoys may result in cardiovascular improvements. Walking seems to be a favorite of many older people and has numerous advantages. It can be done anytime, alone or in a group, with minimal equipment beyond a good pair of shoes. Walking can be misleading—it is so common that it may not seem like exercise at all! Thus, persons new to walking as exercise (and many who have been doing it for some time) may tend to skip the most important steps in an exercise program: warm-ups and cool-downs.

It is critical to warm up slowly, both on a given day and in beginning any new exercise program. Stretching is extremely important both before exercise, to get the muscles ready to work, and after exercise, to help remove lactic acid from the muscles. Neglecting the preexercise warm-up can lead to injury. Neglecting the postexercise cool-down can lead to sore muscles, which in turn can lead to a reluctance to continue the exercise program.

Whatever activity is chosen, whether it be swimming, aerobics, tennis, walking, jogging, weight lifting, or any other, it is important to tailor the activity to the needs and physical condition of the older individual. The person's history, physical abilities, and attitudes toward exercise should be assessed. Personal interests will affect the selection of an activity, as well as one's desire to continue exercising (1, 17).

The benefits of regular exercise cannot be overstated. Regular exercise strengthens the heart and lungs, reduces blood pressure, strengthens bones, and improves muscle tone. These changes occur even with persons who have been sedentary for decades, and within only a few weeks of starting an exercise program. Persons who exercise unanimously report having more energy and sleeping better. Their physical appearance improves, as reported by themselves and their acquaintances, and they indicate improvements in their self-esteem (18, 19). Exercise improves our body's ability to perform when we want it to, thus increasing our sense of control over an important aspect of our lives.

Nutrition

The fuel for exercise, and all body functions, is the food we eat. As persons grow older, there is a modification in level of activity in response to normal physiological changes. This situation is accompanied by a change in nutritional needs. The primary change is a reduction in the amount of food needed for daily functioning. At the same time, the remaining food intake must meet daily nutritional requirements. Hence, there is a great need for older persons to attend to the quality of their food intake (3).

The recommended daily allowance of various food groups, vitamins, and minerals is not constant across the life span. Persons with health concerns and disabilities have further specific nutritional needs at any age. Although nutritional consultants can assist older persons in developing adequate dietary regimens, there is little need for formal assistance for most persons. What is needed is a varied diet that compensates for some of the major age-related changes and health risk factors (1).

Experts recommend a diet high in fiber, which means eating a lot of fresh fruit, cereals, and whole grains. This, combined with adequate fluid intake (the equivalent of eight glasses of water per day), prevents many gastrointestinal disorders among younger as well as older persons. Decreased salt intake is encouraged as persons grow older as one means of preventing cardiovascular diseases. Since taste sensations for salty flavors decrease, aging is accompanied by a natural tendency to increase salt intake to reach former levels of perceived taste sensations. As is true in many areas, planning for aging by reducing salt intake throughout one's adult life is the best preparation in this area.

Vitamin supplements usually are not needed, because most needs can be met through food intake. There is some dispute over whether older women should take calcium supplements. The preponderance of opinion seems to be that calcium can help to prevent osteoporosis when it is taken consistently beginning during menopause. When women wait to begin calcium supplements until well after menopause, such supplements are less effective. In fact, increased calcium intake in the later years actually may aggravate such existing problems as arthritis (1, 15).

The major self-regulatory dietary strategy for maintaining health in the later years seems to be attention to weight. It is important to avoid becoming overweight, especially for those with tendencies toward diabetes and high blood pressure. Excess weight also aggravates arthritic conditions, increasing levels of pain and discomfort. One way to regulate weight is to weigh oneself several times weekly, at the same time of day, and initiate dietary changes at the first sign of weight gain.

Fad diets are not recommended and can in fact be dangerous for some older persons. The key to weight loss while maintaining health is to monitor and moderate one's diet, being sure to achieve the proper intake of various food groups each day. When questions exist as to the proper balance of food groups, a variety of resources exist to provide assistance. In addition to professional nutritional consultants, free information and advice may be obtained from any county agricultural extension agent. Extension offices maintain a supply of free publications on a variety of nutritional topics.

Medication and Diet

Many older persons take medications daily, both over-the-counter and pre-scribed drugs. These medications can alter dietary needs and digestive function-ing (1). It is important to discuss potential changes with physicians, and also with pharmacists, and make any dietary changes needed in order to maximize the effectiveness of the drugs while ensuring that nutritional needs are met. For example, some blood pressure medications deplete dietary potassium, requiring supplemental intake of this mineral through prescription or nutritional intake. Milk products taken along with some antibiotics can neutralize the effects of the drugs. Although these antibiotics should be taken with fruit juice or water, it is important also to get one's daily nutritional need for milk products during the days that one takes antibiotic medications. Thus, milk products are taken at different times of the day, rather than eliminated entirely from the diet.

Some resources for obtaining information to assist older persons in moni-toring their nutritional intake are presented in the last section of this chapter. The goal in all instances is to achieve and maintain good health. When com-bined with a program of exercise, attention to diet can contribute to extreme, positive changes in lifestyle and enjoyment of life at any age. Good physical health sets the stage for enjoyment of life; good mental health also is needed to initiate an active response to life. In effect, each is a necessary but not sufficient condition; it is the interaction of these two areas that ensures quality of life across the life span.

MENTAL HEALTH

Like physical health, mental health is not a static phenomenon. It varies de-pending on the circumstances of life. Aging presents unique challenges to the maintenance of mental health, and unique opportunities for growth and change in positive directions. The many normative physical changes that are part of the aging process are discussed in the preceding sections. All aging persons must adjust to these changes emotionally as well as physically.

There are at least three ways in which physical and mental aging exhibit parallel aspects. First, inactivity has the same impact both physically and mentally. The effect is best summed up in the statement "If you don't use it, you're gonna' lose it." Just as exercise maintains physical strength and health, intellectual and emotional stimulation maintain mental functioning and even improve it. Inactivity, or lack of mental stimulation, leads to functional declines. Over a long period of time, organic brain disorders can result (2).

Second, as implied here, adequate diet is needed to maintain good mental as well as physical functioning. Nutrition is important to the maintenance of mental alertness (1). In addition, intellectual stimulation maintains functioning and increases participation in and enjoyment of life. This is true at any age. There are persons who live active and joyful lives well into their eighth and ninth decades. Death and burial occur at the same time for these persons. Others "die" intellectually in their 30s and 40s, but are not buried until many years later. The latter persons suffer from reduced mental and emotional stimulation and reduced enjoyment of life.

A third parallel between physical and mental functioning may be made in relation to habits and health practices across the life span. In the absence of pathology or disease, sudden changes in mental functioning are not normal. Seemingly sudden changes always must be medically evaluated, immediately. As persons grow older they become more and more like themselves and less and less like other persons. Continuity of personality is normal, as opposed to radical changes based on chronological age (20). Whatever habits have been developed for intellectual stimulation and learning may be expected to continue in the retirement years for most persons.

Certainly the experience of aging is "new" to each individual, and each must prepare for and adjust to a variety of changes and life experiences. Some of these experiences are common to all older people, whereas others are unique. Just as exercise and diet moderate physical health in the later years, there are two key factors that moderate mental health. These include issues of control over one's life and moving toward ego integrity.

Controlling One's Life

Some authors have noted that there are basically two kinds of persons in the world. The first kind perceive themselves as having a high degree of control over the events of their lives. These persons believe in their intrinsic ability to set and achieve goals. The second kind perceives themselves to have little control over the events of their lives. Major goals and decisions are attributed to "fate" or predestiny. The first kind of person is described as having an internal locus of control, the latter as having an external locus of control (21). The difference is in one's perception of who or what is responsible for what happens in one's life. Throughout most of life, most persons feel a sense of control over their daily activities and destinies.

Aging has often been described as a phenomenon of loss—loss of friends through moves, retirements, and death; loss of jobs as a result of retirement; loss of spouse; loss of health; loss of roles; and other losses. Although this is a rather negative view of the later years, there is much truth in this perspective. The danger is that the losses can become the focal point of existence. Since one usually has little or no control over a loss, the normal concomitants of aging can contribute to a sense of loss of control over major aspects of one's life (22).

Persons with an external locus of control may find their basic view of life confirmed by age-related changes. Persons with an internal locus of control may find their basic beliefs in themselves shaken by their experience. Many older persons *learn* that they have increasingly less control over their environment and the events and circumstances of their lives. They are at risk for developing a sense of "learned helplessness' (23), a belief that nothing they do can or will change what is happening to them. The result, similar to lack of physical exercise, is a lowered self-concept (24) and decreasing ability to exercise what control remains. A negative spiral of inactivity (discussed in Chapter 4) accompanied by mental and physical decline can result.

Of course, this negative cycle is not inevitable and certainly may be interrupted and reversed. The key is to develop and maintain a sense of control. Control of one's physical health and lifestyle already have been discussed, and these are important components of an overall sense of control. In addition, control of mental and emotional health is needed. This begins with structuring a safe and healthy personal environment, one in which the older person is free to grow and develop throughout the life span.

Two important aspects of personal safety and growth should be considered. One, the development and maintenance of a support system to enhance personal control and happiness, is discussed in detail in Chapter 6. The second aspect is an internal one, and includes personal habits and attitudes affecting mental health.

Persons who set and achieve goals tend to experience a sense of control. Age, as noted in Chapter 4, does not set a limit on this process. Older persons who continue to set and achieve goals and plan for and work toward their future tend to experience more satisfaction in life. Goals need not be long term, but can be of short-term duration, leading to fairly immediate personal satisfaction. For example, an older person may elect to take a course in painting, satisfying a lifelong curiosity about his or her artistic ability. Another may decide to learn about accounting and take responsibility for submitting his or her own income tax. Another may decide to grow a vegetable garden, another may enjoy dancing, another may golf, another may fish, another may spend increasing amounts of time relaxing with friends in social situations.

The important thing is not what one does, but the purposive nature of one's experiences. Whatever lifestyle and activities are chosen, enjoyment of life is related to the perceived freedom to choose. Even persons with physical disabilities are able to choose many aspects of their lifestyle and environment. When physical infirmities inhibit performance of previous activities, persons can still make a number of personal choices involving their attitudes and reactions.

Good mental health, while related to physical health, can exist in its absence (1, 25). The factors that are important to good mental health are to a great extent independent of physical functioning. These factors, for persons of any age, include an openness to experience, curiosity about life, sense of humor, and eagerness for personal growth and self-expression. Writing, talking, and reading—all are avenues to growth that are possible even when physical declines prevent more active pursuits.

Moving Toward Ego Integrity

Human development is a process. The process begins at conception and proceeds throughout the life span, with varying challenges to growth based on mental, social, and physical developments. Some of the challenges to growth are described as crises, with the major psychosocial crisis of old age being that of integrity versus despair (26). The implication is that older persons will develop in one of two directions: growth or decline.

A universal occurrence in older persons is a phenomenon called the *life review* (27). This is a process of looking back over one's life, remembering and reviewing the events and circumstances of one's life, one's decisions, and the outcomes of those decisions. Many older persons emerge from this process with a sense of fulfillment. If life could be lived again, essentially the same major decisions would be made. There is a feeling that the life one has lived is the best one could have lived—there is a feeling of ego integrity, a serenity and sense of satisfaction with what has been and what is.

Some older persons look back over their lives and regret some of their decisions, and some of the outcomes of those decisions. They may wish they could start over, make some changes, try again. The fact of few remaining years of life makes such changes impossible. Nothing can be done to change what has been, yet they dwell on what could have been and regret what is. These older persons experience a sense of despair. They want to make significant changes in their lives, yet recognize that there is little time or opportunity.

Despair is not inevitable, and it can be changed. Ego integrity also is not inevitable. However, the tendency for most people is to grow in positive, actualizing directions. The sense of control discussed above is important for achieving ego integrity. Whether or not one has direct control over the events in one's life, control over one's reactions is always possible. Persons who view the events of their lives as opportunities for growth and learning will be more open to perceiving their lives in a positive, ego-enhancing manner.

Achieving ego integrity is a process, rather than an outcome. It involves maintaining a personally satisfying level of intellectual and social activity, with adequate time and effort devoted to personal reflection and life review. The process involves a determination of life goals not yet achieved, and setting and achieving those goals that still have meaning and relevance.

IMPLICATIONS FOR COUNSELORS

Mental and physical health are closely interrelated. Changes in one aspect of functioning both affect and are controlled by the other. It is well established that enhancing physical health leads to improved mental health as well. The reverse also is true. When negative attitudes, anger, frustration, and a sense of helplessness are experienced, the resultant stress can lead to poor physical health. Treatment that addresses only one aspect of functioning is destined to be unsuccessful. Holistic approaches are required.

Counselors working with older persons need a variety of types of information in order to be helpful. It is important that they understand the normative aspects of biological aging, as well as common health problems and disabilities, in order to provide accurate information to older clients. Such knowledge can be valuable for counselors as they help older persons understand the changes they are experiencing or will experience, and plan their lives to accommodate them.

Some knowledge of the benefits of exercise and proper diet is essential. Counselors should be able to discuss exercise programs and nutritional needs, but at the same time need to be aware of community resources to meet clients' needs in these areas. Some resources for obtaining additional information about exercise and nutritional programs are included at the end of this chapter. Counselors themselves should have healthy lifestyle habits in order to serve as models to their clients. It is difficult to assist persons in changing physically abusive habits unless counselors also avoid smoking, excessive eating, and so forth.

One area in which counselors can have a large impact in working with older persons is in helping them achieve and recognize a personal sense of control of their lives. Environmental interventions and restructuring may be required, including advocacy with overprotective care providers as well as modifications of the living environment to increase independent functioning. Counselors can help older persons who lack a sense of control to discuss the circumstances of their lives and their emotional reactions. Alternative ways of viewing their circumstances and changes in attitudes and feelings will be likely outcomes of the counseling and exploration processes.

Counselors are trained to facilitate change and growth, and they will find all of their skills useful when helping older persons to review their lives and achieve a sense of ego integrity. Opportunities for life review can be structured in both individual and group counseling settings. Counselors can listen attentively as older persons describe the events and decisions of their lives, and help them focus on the nature and dynamics of their choices rather than just on the outcomes. Awareness of how the circumstances of their lives led them to make the "right" choices at any given point in time can help turn a sense of despair into a feeling of accomplishment. Helping people reframe their life experiences in a positive sense, drawing on and emphasizing strengths, will help older people achieve ego integrity and satisfaction as they view their lives.

GROUP ACTIVITIES

I. Have each person in the group contact one or more of the agencies listed below and obtain information about their services and resources. This information can be shared in a group session. Participants can discuss how the types of information gathered could be used in counseling with older adults.

II. Invite representatives from local exercise and nutrition programs to present information about their services and rationale for their program goals. A panel discussion with questions and answers relating to exercise and diet for older persons can follow the presentation.

Resources for Additional Information

Exercise and fitness programs
  Community agencies
    YMCAs, YWCAs
    Community centers
    Community colleges
    Hospitals
    Parks and recreational facilities
    Senior centers
    Service organizations
    Physicians associations
  Administration on Aging
    Public Information Office (330 C Street S.W., Washington, DC 20202)
  National Institute on Aging
    Exercise (Bldg. 31, Room 5C35, Bethesda, MD 20205)
  Area agencies on aging
  Information and referral programs
Nutrition and diet programs
  All agencies listed above
  Registered Dieticians Association
  Senior nutrition programs
  Bookstores
  County extension offices
Other health programs
  National associations for various diseases and disabilities

(e.g., Arthritis Foundation, National Kidney Foundation, and National Heart and Lung Institute)

REFERENCES

1 Ferrini, A. F., & Ferrini, R. L. (1986). *Health in the later years.* Dubuque, IA: William C. Brown.
2 Butler, R. N., & Lewis, M. I. (1982). Aging and mental health. St. Louis: C. V. Mosby.
3 Saxon, S., & Etten, M. J. (1978). *Physical change and aging: A guide for the helping professions.* New York: Tiresias Press.
4 Lugo, J. O., & Hershey, G. L. (1979). *Human development.* New York: Macmillan.
5 Disfefaro, A. F., & Aston, S. J. (1986). Rehabilitation for the blind and visually impaired elderly. In S. J. Brody & G. E. Ruff (Eds.), *Aging and rehabilitation* (pp. 203–217). New York: Springer.
6 Glass, L. E. (1986). Rehabilitation for deaf and hearing impaired elderly. In S. J. Brody & G. E. Ruff (Eds.), *Aging and rehabilitation* (pp. 218–237). New York: Springer.
7 Willis, S. L., & Baltes, P. B. (1980). Intelligence in adulthood and aging: Contemporary issues. In L. W. Pown (Ed.), *Aging in the 1980s.* (pp. 260–272). Washington, DC: American Psychological Association.
8 Elsenberg, M. G., Sutkin, L. C., & Jansen, M. A. (Eds.). (1984). *Chronic illness and disability through the lifespan.* New York: Springer.
9 Masters, W. H., & Johnson, V. (1968). Human sexual response: The aging female and the aging male. In B. L. Neugarten (Ed.), *Middle-age and aging* (pp. 269–279). Chicago: University of Chicago Press.
10 Cox, H. G. (1988). *Later life: The realities of aging* (2nd ed.). Englewood Cliffs, NJ: Prentice-Hall.
11 Finnerty-Fried, P. F., Myers, J. E., & Barry, J. (1986). Rehabilitation of older persons disabled by cancer, stroke, and heart disease. *Rehabilitation Counseling Bulletin, 29*(4), 266–277.
12 Brotman, H. (1982). *Every ninth American* (Comm. Pub. No. 97-332). Washington, DC: U.S. House of Representatives.
13 Brody, S. J., & Ruff, G. E. (1986). *Aging and rehabilitation: Advances in the state of the art.* New York: Springer.
14 Harris, L., & Associates. (1981). *Aging in the eighties: America in transition.* Washington, DC: National Council on the Aging.
15 Tierny, J. (1982, May). The aging body. *Esquire,* pp. 23–25.
16 Belloc, N. B., & Breslow, L. (1972). Relationship of physical health status and health practices *Preventive Medicine, 1,* 409–421.
17 Pardini, A. (1982, April-May). Exercise, vitality, and aging: *Aging,* pp. 19–29.
18 Glasser, W. (1976). *Positive addiction.* New York: Harper and Row.
19 Hinkle, S. (1988). Psychological benefits of aerobic nursing: Implications for mental health counselors. *American Mental Health Counselors Association Journal, 10*(4), 245–253.

20 Neugarten, B. L. (1968). *Middle-age and aging.* Chicago: University of Chicago Press.
21 Rotter, J. B. (1966). Generalized expectancies for internal versus external control of reinforcement. *Psychological Monographs, 80*(1), 609.
22 Ryckman, R. M., & Malikioski, M. X. (1975). Relationship between locus of control and chronological age. *Psychological Reports, 36,* 655–658.
23 Seligman, L. (1976). *Helplessness: On depression, development, and death.* San Francisco, CA: W. W. Freeman.
24 Reid, D. W., Haas, G., & Hawkins, D. (1977). Locus of designed control and positive self-concept in the elderly. *Journal of Gerontology, 32*(4), 441–450.
25 Myers, J. E. (Ed.). (1981). Rehabilitation of older persons [Special issue], *Journal of Rehabilitation, 47*(4).
26 Erikson, E. (1963). *Childhood and society.* New York: Norton.
27 Butler, R. N. (1963). The life review: An interpretation of reminiscence in the aged. *Psychiatry, 26,* 65–76.

Chapter Six

Relating to Others

Relationships with others are important during all phases of the life span. Interpersonal contacts are the basis for development, maintenance, and enhancement of one's self-concept at virtually any age (1). Persons approaching retirement age face new challenges and often disruptions in the development and maintenance of relationships. Factors such as job change, geographic relocation, death, divorce, and retirement itself may precipitate significant changes in the interpersonal relationships. Some of these changes are desirable, whereas others, which may not be wanted, lie beyond the control of the older person.

In Chapter 5 we examined personal health habits and their relationships to good mental and physical health during retirement. In Chapter 7, work and leisure activities are considered as they relate to the lifestyles of healthy and fully functioning persons. In this chapter, the vital nature of interpersonal relationships for retirees is considered. The first section reviews essential factors in relationships with others. The next five sections address factors in the retiree's relationships with his or her spouse, children and grandchildren, friends and neighbors, former work associates, and aging parents and other family members. Implications for counselors are discussed. The Group Activities section focuses on the importance of support networks.

ESSENTIAL FACTORS IN RELATING TO OTHERS

Three factors are essential for establishing satisfactory relationships with others: first, older persons' positive feelings about themselves; second, their positive points of view toward other persons; and third, quality communications, both verbal and nonverbal.

In Chapter 4, the appreciation of oneself and the importance of regarding oneself as a worthy person were emphasized. A positive approach to life and living was underscored. Qualities like these help to create a favorable climate wherein satisfactory relationships can develop. A person with these qualities is regarded as a pleasure to meet.

Further, these persons have an additional contribution to make to a relationship: They regard other persons as also worthy and as providing, potentially at least, windows into their own worlds that have much of value to offer. One example is an 80-year-old widow whose interest in other people brought her their affection and appreciation wherever she went. In a restaurant one evening she noticed that her waitress seemed sad. Upon inquiry, she learned that the waitress's little girl was in the hospital. The widow expressed concern, but in addition, she purchased a teddy bear that she gave to the waitress for her child several evenings later.

The third essential factor in developing a relationship is the quality of the communications, verbal and nonverbal. Thompson and Nusbaum (2, p. 96) have suggested that "communication not only defines, creates, and reflects relationships, but that communication *is* the relationship."

Simply stated, communications consist of the words spoken and the feelings expressed, by the voice, by facial expressions, and by body language. If the words, the tone of voice, and the body language convey mixed messages— some favorable, some unfavorable—persons receiving these messages can become confused, perhaps distrustful. Therefore, it becomes important for the communicator to be clear about the message to be sent, to choose his or her words carefully, and to transmit feelings that support the words used.

Communicating effectively is a quality worth cultivating. It is a quality developed through careful practice. It reflects the honesty and forthrightness of the communicator who represents all three factors essential for building a satisfactory relationship. When the person receiving the communication also reflects the same three factors, a rewarding relationship is usually assured.

Effective communications are a significant issue to older persons for several reasons (3). First, successful adaptation to life changes, including development of a helpful support network, may depend in considerable measure on their skills in communicating. Second, the quality of their relationships with both family and friends may be defined by the quality of their communications. Third, communications may help to fill the gap in older persons' participation in various activities caused by reduced mobility. And fourth, communication is a means for raising awareness by adult children and others of older persons' needs.

Faulty communications can lead to deteriorating relationships between a surviving parent and adult children. To illustrate, a mother living with her son and his family seldom left the house, believing that her son was apprehensive when she did so. On the other hand, the son and his wife resented the fact that the mother refused to go out of the house when encouraged to do so. The problem of growing estrangement was resolved when a counselor, at the request of the son, had an opportunity to discuss the problem of relationships with all parties concerned. The problem was the absence of open communications.

IMPORTANCE OF RELATIONSHIPS WITH OTHERS

One way to view relationships with others is in terms of support networks or support systems. These are combinations of interpersonal resources that help meet one's needs. Waters, Weaver, and White (4) suggested two primary categories of support that these systems provide. The first is aimed at helping a person get something done, such as overcoming major problems, obtaining needed services, or gaining information to deal with difficult situations. The second type of support is aimed at meeting universal needs for companionship, caring, and intimacy. The first type is referred to as a *formal* support network, while the second is an *informal* support network.

Formal support networks include all of the professional and community resources that may be mobilized to help older persons meet any of their daily living needs. A broad array of community agencies and services may comprise the formal support network of a given individual. Since the number of possible agencies is large, some mechanism for linking persons with needed services is desirable. Information and referral agencies have the function of providing needed links. They maintain community resource directories and provide referral information as needed. Formal support networks for any given person may change as his or her needs change.

Informal support systems also may change, but these tend to remain stable over long periods of time. Informal supports include the network of family, friends, and neighbors with whom an individual interacts. Support within the informal system is both given and received. One of the characteristics of informal supports is the frequency and emotional depth of interpersonal contacts.

Studies of the nature of life satisfaction among older persons consistently have depicted the informal support network as one of the major correlates of high morale, or a feeling of positive well-being (5). Flanagan (6), in a major study of informal supports, studied quality of life indicators across the life span for a sample of older persons. His study found that for men, the major indicators of quality of life were a spouse and children, in that order. For women, the major quality of life indicators were children and then a spouse.

A landmark piece of research by Lowenthal and Haven (7) revealed that the presence of a single confidant in the life of an older person was the major factor that mitigated against the losses and stresses of aging. Just one person whom an older person felt close to, cared for by, and cared for in return made the difference between life satisfaction and nonsatisfaction in the later years. That person could be anyone—spouse, sibling, child, parent, neighbor, friend, or even counselor.

Many persons live their lives with rich and varied informal support networks. These persons may have and maintain contact with many members of their families, may interact with neighbors on a regular basis, and/or may have a strong network of friends and acquaintances with whom they share their time and talents. Other persons live with only one or a few persons with whom they have close emotional contacts. Although loss of loved ones is traumatic for all persons, the loss of any one component, or sometimes *the* component of a small informal support network, can be both devastating and overwhelming.

The discussion at the end of this chapter includes suggestions and strategies for counselors to use to help persons identify the components of their support networks and develop additional supports to meet their current and future needs. Planning for one's personal supports is an important and integral part of a holistic approach to retirement planning. The sections that follow address various components of the informal system, with suggestions for increasing the quality of interactions and life satisfaction in the later years.

RELATING TO ONE'S SPOUSE

Statistics show that three of four older men are married, whereas only one in three older women is married. Widowhood is the predominant reason for "singlehood" in old age, with persons who have never married and those who are separated or divorced comprising small but increasing minorities. The existence of greater numbers of women than men limits access to partners for women, while creating multiple opportunities for older men (8). For those older persons who are married or living with a partner, relating to one another may be discussed in terms of two major situations: when both spouses are fairly healthy, which is the usual situation with older couples, and when one spouse is ill or in poor health.

Enjoying health is discussed in Chapter 5, with the conclusion that most older persons may enjoy good mental and physical health throughout most or all of their lives. So, most older couples will be found to enjoy reasonably good health and be able to continue or vary their lifestyles as they choose, within the limitations of their personal choices and resources. Some changes inevitably accompany advancing years, and changes in lifestyles brought about by retirement can be a mixed blessing. Retirement can be a crisis in the meaningful use of time (9) and potentially a crisis in the meaningful continuation of relationships.

Couples who plan for the changes in their relationship prior to retirement make better and faster adjustments than those who fail to plan. Planning in this instance refers to talking—open communication regarding expectations and plans for each person as an individual, for their spouse, and for their anticipated relationship as a couple. Part of such planning will involve decisions on where to live and preferred leisure activities to pursue. In addition, some attention to legal and financial issues, as discussed in Chapter 9, is important.

Retirement generally provides the opportunity to spend more time together doing things as a couple. Many couples eagerly anticipate the opportunity to spend time together and delight in making plans for travel, home improvements, visits with family and friends, and any number of leisure-time pursuits. Other couples find that the increased amount of time they have together is a burden. Personal lifestyles are disrupted, especially for the woman who has been a homemaker, and the sharing of previously unshared tasks may become increasingly annoying. In contrast, the most difficult time for husbands seems to be when they are anticipating retirement (10).

It is important for couples to take time to talk about their concerns and plans both before and after retirement. For example, a daughter was discussing with her 80-year-old parents some of the situations they would have liked to change in their lives. The mother spoke with some hesitation about her past desire to travel. The father responded, "Why didn't you say you'd like to travel?" His wife replied, "Because I thought you didn't want to travel."

Each should encourage the other to continue to grow and develop as an individual, while also planning activities to participate in as a couple. Both kinds of activities are needed: activities each spouse can participate in alone or with other friends, and activities in which they can participate as a couple. The establishment of routines may be helpful, especially when one spouse suddenly is confronted with a large amount of free time after retiring from a full-time job.

When free time and/or routines are interrupted for health reasons, caretaking responsibilities may disrupt the couple's relationship. The disruption may be short or long. For many older persons, the death of a spouse is preceded by some length of illness, during which the surviving spouse is the caretaker. Relationships may be strained and/or disrupted during these times. Time away from one another spent with friends and pursuing personal hobbies may be limited or eliminated completely in the absence of respite care (11). It is advisable for older couples to seek assistance early after the onset of an illness, rather than waiting until difficulties escalate to the point of angry or resentful feelings. Mobilizing both formal and informal supports can help alleviate the stresses experienced by the caretaking spouse, and help maintain the couple relationship as one of mutual support and caring. Children can be a major source of assistance and both material and emotional support at such times (12).

RELATING TO CHILDREN

Various social trends seem to have affected the relationships of older persons with family members: the number of surviving children, the four-generation family, divorce and remarriage, and the employment of women in the labor force (13). If there are more children, there tends to be greater contact between generations. The appearance of four-generation families means that more older persons have great grandchildren. In addition, older persons nearing retirement age may have responsibilities for their older parents.

Since greater numbers of retirees are likely to have been divorced and remarried, they may experience more financial and emotional problems. With more women employed, those with older parents have less time to be of assistance. In view of these trends, it would seem that the strength of relationships between generations may lie in feelings of mutual independence, economically and psychologically. It would appear that the family's principal purpose, in terms of older members, will be to give psychological support.

Children can be a source of both delight and dismay during the retirement years. Since relationships with them are lifelong, aging parents may expect some stability in the way they relate to their children in the later years. Existing difficulties in communication will not magically disappear, new difficulties may arise, and even the best of relationships may become stressed as a result of retirement.

Problems between older parents and adult children include children's unwillingness to accept their own aging as well as the aging of their parents, the inability of both to shift roles, and sometimes a lack of ability to develop a new set of relationships based on changing life circumstances (14).

An important requirement for retirees is to be aware of time constraints experienced by other persons, especially their children. An abundance of free time for retirees may not be matched by the life situations of their children. This problem can be manifested in at least two ways. Children may "assume" their retired parents would like nothing better than to spend lots of their free time with grandchildren. This may or may not be the case. On the other hand, retirees may attempt to fill their days by spending increasing amounts of time with their adult children, a luxury that was previously denied them because of work schedules. Either of these situations can lead to frustration for all involved. The key to managing them is communication.

Part of planning for retirement may involve planning with other members of the family, including children. Retirees will benefit from being clear in discussing with their children any expectations for their relationships during retirement. Children may do the same. Sharing leisure-time activities and travel with children can be highly enjoyable for all involved (12).

Conflicts can arise between retired persons and their adult children from any number of sources. Already mentioned were lifetime patterns and styles of relating. These can become especially troublesome during times of stress, such as stresses resulting from illness and caretaking responsibilities placed on the children. Research indicates that adult children, especially daughters, are called on to be caretakers for older parents (11). In the absence of needed respite, negative emotions may escalate to the point of abuse (12). Clearly, both advance planning and mobilization of formal support services can help to minimize difficulties for all involved.

Conflicts may arise over needs for independence, usually with adult children becoming overprotective of their parents. Being members of a society that negatively stereotypes older persons, the reactions or overreactions of adult children are sometimes understandable. Sometimes they even are justified. When disability is present, the attentions of adult children can either magnify or reduce difficulties for the older person. When older persons resist these attentions, however, it most likely is because the children are overreacting and the older persons simply do not require assistance. Again, open communication can help to alleviate difficult situations, though outside intervention may sometimes be needed. An independent advocate can help both adult children and aging parents recognize when their reactions are inappropriate or even destructive.

Recent years and increased life spans have created a new conflict of needs for independence: adult children expect parents to fit into the younger family's lifestyle. This can mean spending vacations together, traveling together, or simply spending time with children and grandchildren. Older persons usually want to continue being independent persons, just as they have for their own adult lives. Their preferences and activity schedules may mean that they simply are not available when adult children want them to be. Moreover, they are not available "on call," as children discover when they call Mom or Dad to invite their participation in some event. As one of the authors has found in a variety of workshops, counseling situations, and other personal conversations, this conflict is a source of distress and can be extremely painful, especially for adult children. Quite simply, they interpret their parent's lack of availability as rejection, with the concomitant negative emotions that accompany rejection experiences (12).

One of the keys to maintaining good relationships with family members in the later years is to accord them the same relationship privileges as one provides to friends. This point of view is true for both aging parents and their adult children. Some strategies for dealing with friends are discussed in the following section.

LOSING AND GAINING FRIENDS

Actor George Burns is reported to have said that the best thing about turning 80 is that there isn't much peer pressure! Certainly one of the facts of advancing age is the loss of significant others in one's life. These include friends, both casual and close, recent and long standing. Though many losses occur because of death or disability that removes friends from their home to an institutional setting, perhaps at some distance, losses of close relationships also are precipitated by moves. Older persons may move, their friends or neighbors may move, or both may move when neighborhoods are renovated or destroyed in favor of needed highways or shopping malls. Many older persons move to be closer to their children or grandchildren.

Regardless of the reasons for the loss, some attention to grief work is necessary. This means that older persons must come to terms emotionally with each loss, and take time to process their feelings of grief or abandonment (in severe cases). The final stage of grief is a resolution, a new growth, and a move toward replacement of at least some of the functions the lost person filled in one's life (15). In the absence of healthy grieving, personal growth will not occur.

Those older persons who have only one or a few close personal friends will be most incapacitated by their loss and resulting grief. Those who plan their lives to have broad and varied support networks still will grieve each loss, but at the same time will have a greater array of personal resources to assist with their grieving and eventual reintegration and growth. Having friends and acquaintances in each age group across the life span is one way to assure a broad network of supportive friends to cope with losses. Such a support network also presents a means of contact for redeveloping aspects of one's support system which are lost (16).

It is as true for older persons as for persons of any age that they meet people they like doing things they like to do. Common activities and interests are the basis for long and enjoyable friendships. For those persons who like to join groups, group memberships can be a viable means of meeting like-minded individuals. Persons who prefer solitary activities may have more difficulty meeting persons with whom to share their time. Local senior centers and clubs and programs for older persons can help fill the gap in social contacts for older persons who experience losses of friends and neighbors.

McGinnis (17) has listed several suggestions for establishing friendships: (a) Be cautious in criticizing others; (b) communicate acceptance rather than approval or disapproval of another's behavior; (c) encourage others to be unique, to be themselves; (d) allow others time to be alone; (e) encourage people to make other friendships; and (f) be prepared for shifts in relationships and priorities. Friendship is a voluntary phenomenon. Whether friends are relatives or unrelated persons, adhering to basic principles of mutual respect can help to establish and maintain friendships across the life span.

RELATING TO FORMER WORK ASSOCIATES

Once a person retires, former work associates become potentially and can remain just friends. Whether they actually are one's friends depends on a number of factors. If a co-worker was a friend prior to retirement, he or she is much more likely to be a friend during one's retirement. If a co-worker was not a particularly close friend during the work years, when there are no longer shared activities in retirement friendly relationships are not likely to be continued. Continuity of relationships is the safest thing to expect—what existed before may continue, but closer relationships are unlikely to develop.

Again, shared activities are the source of many friendships. When a person retires, the shared activity at work terminates, though friendships may continue. Maintaining friendships with former co-workers requires the retiree to retain a sense of and respect for the co-worker's time constraints. Trying to make them take ever longer lunch breaks to fill the retiree's time will cause co-workers to avoid the company of their former companions. Successful friendships build on an existing foundation. If relationships were structured around work topics and work schedules, attempts to keep those relationships active must occur within a new and different structure.

Maintaining relationships with previous co-workers can be enjoyable and can help people retain a sense of continuity after retirement. Time spent in learning about new developments and continuing activities in the former work site can help retirees feel still somewhat involved in their work life. Not everyone desires this. Often retirees gradually come to recognize an increasing distance between their daily lives in retirement and their former work lives. If friendships with former work associates are to be maintained, it is important to structure other than work activities that are mutually satisfying. Talking about work may be part of the relationship, but growth and development of any relationship requires new activities for the participation and involvement of both persons. These guidelines for maintaining friendships mentioned above will be useful in dealing with former work associates who, after retirement, may best be classified as past, current, or potential friends.

RELATING TO AGING PARENTS AND OTHER FAMILY MEMBERS

Many persons today are members of three- or four-generation families. Thus, many retirees will find that their parents are still living. As is true for their relationships with children, retirees have an opportunity to relate to their parents as friends, and to share travel and leisure pursuits with them. There are many opportunities to relate to and learn from each other. For example, projects such as developing shared family histories can facilitate the life review process for retirees and their parents. Older persons can share strategies for adjusting to and learning to enjoy various aspects of retirement.

When older parents become ill or disabled, it is often the retired adult child who becomes a caretaker or care arranger (19). As mentioned earlier, this can be a stressful experience at any age, and arrangements for respite care are essential. Mobilizing the resources of other family members also may be necessary, ranging from children to grandchildren to siblings, nieces, nephews, or cousins. Family members can provide material or financial support, and frequently are sources of needed emotional support.

Siblings are an increasingly valuable source of support for many older persons. Rivalries and disagreements of earlier years tend to become less important with advancing age. Siblings can be a source of great pleasure and close friendship, and should be treated with the respect and care provided friends who are nonrelatives. Arranging for leisure activities together, sharing caretaking responsibilities, and planning joint projects all can be rewarding for family members. Sharing can contribute to strengthening of family ties, thus increasing the support network and positive emotions of all family members, even in times of stress. Family members who develop habits of supporting and encouraging one another are better able to cope with stress without needing outside interventions. Those who must look outside of their family for support may find the services of professional counselors increasingly useful in dealing with difficulties that arise in the retirement years.

IMPLICATIONS FOR COUNSELORS

Support systems are not static, but rather continually change over the course of a lifetime. Because they are so vitally important for maintaining health and life satisfaction, counselors must be prepared for at least three functions is working with retirees. These include analyzing support networks, enhancing existing supports, and helping retirees to analyze their support networks and develop needed personal and interpersonal resources.

Analyzing support networks may be approached in a number of different ways. Waters et al. (4) used a needs assessment approach to support systems and provided a worksheet for assessing existing needs and gaps. The worksheet asks respondents to consider a series of possible needs, the type of support that typically might meet that need, and their own source of support for meeting that need, if any. Salmon (16) used a pictorial Gestalt approach to help persons identify strong, distant, and conflicting sources of support in their lives. Ashinger (18) employed a similar approach, called the Social Network Inventory. Again a pictorial representation of resources is developed to help persons identify existing and needed supports in their lives. Ashinger estimated that each person will identify an average of 40 supportive contacts in a 1-year time period, which may be greatly overestimated for many retired persons. Each of these methods can be used in working with retirees to help them analyze and identify the components of their support systems.

Where gaps in support networks exist, counselors can play a vital role in helping retirees develop resources to meet their needs. It is important to remember that people do not like to ask for help; nor are they always willing to accept help when it is needed or offered. Recognizing the need for assistance, finding resources to meet such needs, and accepting needed assistance may be difficult for some retirees, yet these things are made easier through counseling interventions. Counselors can help retirees explore their needs and resources, and emotional reactions to both. Where needed resources are lacking, counselors can help retirees develop plans for obtaining those resources, and may even act as advocates for their older clients.

Clearly, it is important for counselors to be aware of existing resources and community services to fill gaps in the personal resource base of their clients. These resources and services include recreational and social opportunities, as well as medical, financial, housing, legal, and other means of formal assistance. Direct referral and advocacy may be required. In addition, interventions with family members and caregivers can help to alleviate stress and improve interpersonal relationships for retirees and their existing support persons. Counselors will find many challenges in dealing with family members, including habits and relationship patterns that, though self-defeating, have developed and solidified over half a century or more. Skills in relating to individuals and groups will be critically important for counselors wanting to enhance support networks of retired persons.

GROUP ACTIVITIES

Try to identify the various components of your own support system.
1   First, draw three columns on a sheet of clean paper.
   A   The first column should be titled Past Supports, the second Current Supports, and the third Future Support.
   B   Begin by filling in the middle column with Current Supports. Start by listing formal supports, which would include any relationships or interactions with institutions and agencies. Then, list those persons who affect your life, including spouse or partner, children, friends, work associates, and parents and other family members. The last entries should include activities that form an important part of your personal support system, such as hobbies and exercise programs, pet care, etc. When the list is complete, look back over it and mark a + or − beside each support depending on whether it is important and positive or somewhat conflicting or negative in your life.

   C In the first column, list supports that were important to you 10 (or 20 or 30) years ago, and in the third column list the supports that you believe will be important to you 10 (or 20 or 30) years in the future. Try to project who and what your sources of support will be in the future.

2 Compare the three columns. What do they suggest about the changing nature of support systems?

3 Discuss your support systems in small groups of three to five persons. What are the commonalities and differences in support that each of you identified? What are the major differences between your second and third column? How can you plan to make the third column as desirable as possible?

4 Discuss your overall reactions to this exercise in a large group prior to the end of your session.

REFERENCES

1 Rogers, C. (1961). *On becoming a person.* Boston: Houghton Mifflin.

2 Thompson, T. L., & Nussbaum, J. F. (1988). Interpersonal communication. In C. W. Carmichael, C. H. Botan, & R. Hawkins (Eds.), *Human communication and the aging process* (pp. 95–109). Prospect Heights, IL: Waveland Press.

3 Nussbaum, J. F., Thompson, T. L., & Robinson, J. D. (1989). *Communication and aging.* New York: Harper and Row.

4 Waters, E., Weaver, A., & White, J. (1981). Specialized techniques to help older people. In J. E. Myers (Ed.), *Counseling older persons: Volume 3. A trainer's manual for basic helping skills* (pp. 147–169). Alexandria, VA: American Association for Counseling and Development.

5 Lohmann, N. (1977). Correlations of life satisfaction, morale, and adjustment measures. *Journal of Gerontology, 32*(3), 73–75.

6 Flanagan, J. C. (1982). *New insights to improve the quality of life at age 70.* Palo Alto, CA: American Institute for Research in the Behavioral Sciences.

7 Lowenthal, M. F., & Haven, F. C. (1968). Interaction and adaptation: Intimacy as a critical variable. In B. L. Neugarten (Ed.), *Middle age and aging* (pp. 390–400). Chicago, IL: University of Chicago Press.

8 Butler, R. N., & Lewis, M. I. (1982). *Aging and mental health.* St. Louis: C. V. Mosby.

9 Havighurst, R. J. (1961). The nature and values of meaningful free time activity. In R. J. Kleemeier (Ed.), *Aging and leisure* (pp. 338–343). New York: Oxford University.

10 Cox, H. E. (1988). *Later life: The realities of aging.* Englewood Cliffs, NJ: Prentice-Hall.

11 Sommers, T., & Shields, L. (1987). *Women take care: The consequences of caregiving in today's society.* Gainesville, FL: Triad.

12 Myers, J. E. (1989). *Counseling adult children and aging parents.* Alexandria, VA: American Association for Counseling and Development.

13 National Institute on Aging, U. S. Department of Health and Human Services. (1981). *Aging and the family.* (Prepared for the 1981 White House Conference on Aging). Washington, DC.

14 Silverstone, B., & Hyman, H. K. (1976). *You and your aging parent.* New York: Pantheon Books.

15 Kubler-Ross, E. (1975). *Death: The final stage of growth.* Englewood Cliffs, NJ: Prentice-Hall.

16 Salmon, H. (1981). How can I make the best use of support networks? In J. E. Myers (Ed.), *Counseling older persons: Vol. 3. A trainer's manual for basic helping skills* (pp. 183-195). Alexandria, VA: American Association for Counseling and Development.

17 McGinnis, A. L. (1979). *The friendship factor.* Minneapolis, MN: Augsburg Press.

18 Ashinger, P. (1985). Using social networks in counseling. *Journal of Counseling and Development, 63,* 519-521.

19 Matthews, S. H. (1987). Provision of care to old parents: Division of responsibility among adult children. *Research on Aging, 9*(1), 45-60.

Chapter Seven

Making Use of Time

Retirement has been called a "crisis in the meaningful use of time" (1, p. 338). Although ideally retirement is a process of moving from some important things to other important things, for many persons it represents a challenge in time management different from any other they have experienced. For most persons, life has always been "managed," and time has always been allocated for major tasks and activities, more or less automatically.

One's work life may extend some 40–50 years, during which many aspects of daily living become fairly routine, such as preparing for work, getting to and from work, adjusting to set times for work and leisure, and so forth. It is easy to become complacent about time management. Retirement disrupts the routines, leaving many to answer the question: "What do I do now?"

Loss of the work role at retirement creates a crisis in self-definition as well as time usage. Some attention to time usage and time structure can significantly reduce the impact of these crises. The key is to recognize the needs that were met by work, then determine where and how these needs may be met after retirement (2). For some persons, continuing to work is the primary choice for meeting one or more of these needs. For others, careful planning of time usage with attention to leisure pursuits is vital.

This chapter begins with an overview of the importance of work and the role of worker. In the sections that follow, options for employment (paid or volunteer), leisure, and learning are discussed. The importance of striving for a reasonable balance in activities and time management is reviewed, followed by implications for counselors.

IMPORTANCE OF WORK AND THE ROLE OF WORKER

In response to the question "What do I do now?", one retired man answered by designing a business card worded as follows:

No plans	No connections
No problems	No responsibilities
	John M. Doe
	Retired
No business	No money
No worries	No prospects
	No telephone

In its lack of structure, this business card serves an important function, namely identification of who one is and what one's purpose in life (or lack thereof!) may be. In effect, not working is this retired person's "work." The Protestant work ethic still is the major influence on personal definitions of work in our society (3). Statements such as the following reflect the dominant cultural values:

"Without work, all life goes rotten." (Albert Camus)
"When people are serving, life is no longer meaningless." (John Gardner)
"A man is a worker. If he is not that he is nothing." (Joseph Conrad)
"It is not enough to be busy. The question is: what are we busy about?" (Henry David Thoreau)

Work values have been widely studied, with the conclusion that work serves a variety of important functions for individuals (4, 5). These may be summarized in five areas: status, socialization, income, time structure, and self-esteem.

The type of work one does and even the fact that one is employed are sources of status and esteem. A variety of studies have attempted to rate professions and occupations according to the esteem in which they are held by the general public. Public newspapers and other media occasionally publish the results. Consistently, occupations such as physician, dentist, pilot, lawyer, banker, and college professor top the list of high-status occupations. The most common question asked when meeting new persons, after (but not always) their name, is "What do you do?" The answer establishes the level of esteem in which the new acquaintance is held.

When one is introduced as a surgeon, for example, persons immediately conjure an image of a high-status person and may inquire as to the medical specialty and type of practice. If, on the other hand, a person introduces him- or herself as a retired surgeon, little occurs in the way of spontaneous questioning from that point on. The level of status has been significantly reduced when the job description is modified with the word *retired*. Perhaps in this context, as in many others, retirement is viewed as a noun, rather than a verb. It implies no action, therefore no discussion is necessary.

The choice of one's job in a sense dictates one's social life and lifestyle (6). Most persons socialize with others of similar status, with status being defined by one's work. People tend to share interests and socialize with co-workers, for example, and co-workers tend to share the same socioeconomic means. The choice of job directly affects the persons with whom one comes in contact for one-third or more of each working day. Since these are the people one gets to know, they tend to be the ones to share nonwork time with as well.

Income is directly related to the work one performs. Income affects lifestyle, including choice of housing type and location, style and manner of dress, choice of recreational pursuits, and choice of automobile, to name a few. These choices in turn become indicators of status to other people. Hence, lifestyle is dictated by income, which is dictated by work. Few persons, perhaps less than 5%, choose a lifestyle and then find an occupation which will result in that lifestyle. Most persons choose an occupation and that choice determines their subsequent lifestyle.

Time structure is a fourth variable directly determined by one's choice of work. Most people work according to a time schedule, set either by themselves or others. The 40-hr workweek has been the standard for several decades. Within that week, 8:00 or 9:00 to 5:00 are the standard hours. Some people work rotating, swing, or night shifts that limit their access to services based on the "normal" 40-hr workweek. Anyone who has tried to find a restaurant open for dinner after getting off from the 4:00 to midnight shift is well aware of the limited choices available at that hour.

Work also structures personal time to meet work requirements. Everyone needs a certain amount of sleep before work; time to clean, eat, and dress for work; time to travel to and from the work site; and so forth. These various uses of time related to work create a daily schedule of activities. Nonwork times are specified as well in this schema. Retirement creates an abrupt end to these clearly defined time structures.

Last, but certainly of great importance, is the impact of work on self-esteem. Work provides a sense of meaning and purpose. These feelings often are related to the product of one's work, hence the contribution of a sense of *productivity* to one's feelings of self-worth. All of the functions of work mentioned above also contribute to a sense of self-worth. For example, people feel good or bad about the status of their jobs. The "I'm justa [clerk, waitress, teacher, etc.]" syndrome is an example of the pervasive influence of job title on one's personal sense of status and esteem.

Work can be a major source of life satisfaction or unhappiness. Some jobs, such as air traffic controller, produce more anxiety than others, and some, such as chemists and female physicians, have been linked to higher suicide rates (6). On the other hand, Palmore (7) found work satisfaction to be the best predictor of longevity. Satisfaction with a job or career can change over the course of the life span, and may vary according to occupational life stage.

Many developmental theorists have attempted to describe occupational life cycle stages. For example, Super (8, 9) noted four primary vocational stages: selection and entry, adjustment, maintenance, and retirement. Kimmel (10) maintained that persons in midlife are acutely aware of the time remaining in their lives before retirement and the speed with which they are reaching (or not reaching) their goals.

Given the salience of work, retirement is a major turning point in the occupational life cycle as well as in the adult life span (6). Atchley (11) considered retirement as a central developmental task, at once a process, social role, and phase of life. For Erikson, retirement signified a transition in development from the crisis of generativity versus stagnation to that of ego integrity versus despair.

Given the importance of the work role, many retirees choose to continue working in some capacity. Other choose to work to supplement retirement incomes. A variety of options for employment during the retirement years are discussed in the following section.

CONTINUING EMPLOYMENT

A variety of employment options exist for those older persons who would like to continue working after retirement. The decision to pursue employment should include some consideration for part- versus full-time work. One important choice is whether to continue in the same line of work or seek employment in new areas. Options include both paid and unpaid or volunteer work, employment through special programs serving older workers, employment in the competitive labor market, and self-employment. Each of these possibilities is discussed below, along with barriers and incentives to labor force participation by older workers.

New Career or Old Career?

Retirees who choose to continue working also can choose to work in the same or a new field. Work in one's preretirement field has certain advantages, both for the retiree and for employers. Little or no training is required, and the retiree can bring a significant amount of expertise to work tasks. The retiree can assist in training new employees, solving problems, and so forth.

On the other hand, older workers can be retrained for new jobs within their same field or industry. Employers may choose to retrain and retain older workers rather than lose the valuable resources they represent (12-14). Flexible employer policies can create a variety of opportunities for full- or part-time continuing employment for older workers (15, 16).

On the other hand, retirement presents options for learning new careers, for trying out new job roles, and for exploring different job possibilities (17). Retirees can try to carry out their dreams, from any point in life, of working in new job arenas. Additional training may be required, and the training process itself can be stimulating and exciting. Options for retraining and additional education are discussed in a later section.

Volunteer or Paid Work?

Unpaid or volunteer work is the choice of many but by no means all, or even a majority of, retired persons. About 23% of all older persons engage in volunteer work and another 10% report that they would like to do so. Some 28% of persons aged 65-69 engage in volunteerism, 23% of persons aged 70-79 do so, and 12% of those aged 80 and above (18).

There may be differences in volunteerism among older persons on the basis of factors such as socioeconomic status or previous employment. In a recent study of retirees by the Teachers Insurance and Annuity Association, College Retirement Equity Fund (TIAA-CREF), for example, half of the respondents reported performing volunteer or charitable service (19). Many reported that volunteer work gave them the opportunity to devote unused talents to some pursuit previously impossible because of the time constraints imposed by work. Women were more likely than men to engage in volunteer activities, with 60% of women (70% of single women) and 45% of men doing so. The major philanthropic efforts of the TIAA-CREF retirees were as follows: community and civic groups (e.g., United Way, Boy Scouts), 28%; educational/cultural services (e.g., Headstart, museum, library), 27%; church, synagogue, religious organizations, 27%; hospital and health services, 15%; helping older persons (e.g., Meals on Wheels, senior center aide); and other (e.g., government agencies, election polls), 14%. Many retirees engaged in more than one type of volunteer activity.

Popular stereotypes of the older person with ample time on his or her hands eager to perform any available volunteer activity are quite untrue. As at any other time of life, for older persons the best predictor of future behavior is past performance. Those persons who have been active as volunteers throughout their adult lives will be most likely to continue to participate as volunteers during their retirement years. Those persons who have not typically volunteered their time cannot be expected suddenly to want to work for no pay when they have a 40- to 50-year history of paid work experiences.

Those older persons who choose to volunteer their time will find ample opportunities to do so in any community. Volunteer work can be in their area of specialty or expertise, such as volunteering in the industry or work setting in which they worked prior to retirement. Usually this is not a good option, since work for no pay in the environment where one once worked for pay creates cognitive dissonance and potentially has a negative impact on self-esteem. Acting as a consultant, rather than a worker per se, places the retiree in a position of status, and will make volunteer activities within prior work settings or work areas more challenging and enjoyable.

Many retirees volunteer for community service work activities. These can range from serving on volunteer advisory boards to working with youth or physically ill or disabled children and adults, to assisting in city beautification programs. Some volunteer opportunities are designed specifically for older persons. These are discussed in the next section, since they often include some reimbursement for travel and/or time and effort.

The decision to engage in volunteer as opposed to paid work is a highly individual one. Some older persons want or need to supplement their incomes and hence prefer work for pay. Others enjoy the freedom provided by part-time volunteer work. For some, volunteer work is an important commitment with the same value paid work and for many of the same reasons (e.g., time schedule, sense of responsibility, job tasks). Many persons look forward to increased community service through volunteerism as they grow older. For them, status accrues from having the freedom and desire to help others. Other older persons do not value volunteer roles and would not consider work without pay, even a token salary.

Employment Through Older Worker Programs

The federal government has developed and encouraged a number of employment programs for older workers (20, 21). Most of these are coordinated at the state level through area agencies on aging and state units on aging. Agencies serving older persons are encouraged to give preference to hiring persons over 60 for staff positions. Other older worker employment programs are operated under the auspices of sheltered workshops and other rehabilitation agencies designed to serve the needs of persons with disabilities (22).

The most well-known federally funded programs for older workers are those under the ACTION agency, which is the federal volunteer agency (20). There are five ACTION programs.

The Foster Grandparent Program offers low-income older persons the opportunity to provide attention and care to physically, mentally, and emotionally handicapped children in institutions and community settings. Foster grandparents typically work half a day 4 days a week. They receive training, travel expenses, annual physical examinations, and a very small stipend.

The Retired Senior Volunteer Program provides persons over age 60 with a variety of work experiences in agencies, organizations, schools, and institutions in their communities. They receive on-the-job training as needed, travel expenses, and meals.

VISTA, Volunteers in Service to America, is a national corps of persons of all ages who agree to work for a minimum of 1 year in impoverished areas. Volunteers receive training, a monthly food and housing allowance, and a small stipend for incidentals.

The Peace Corps recruits both younger and older persons to serve for a minimum of 2 years in overseas positions to help developing nations. A 3-month training program is held, transportation is provided to the country assigned, and a monthly allowance for food, travel, and housing is provided. All medical needs are also provided.

The Senior Companion Program is similar to the Foster Grandparent Program. Volunteers work with impaired adults and older persons in their homes and in institutional settings. Any needed training, a travel and meals allowance, and annual physical examination are provided through the program.

In addition to the ACTION programs, several other federal agencies sponsor older worker programs. The Small Business Administration sponsors SCORE, the Service Corps of Retired Executives. SCORE links older persons who have management expertise with owners and managers of small businesses and community organizations. SCORE counselors or consultants may be reimbursed for expenses.

The Department of Labor administers the Senior Community Service Employment Program, which is authorized by Title IX of the Older Americans Act. This program places older persons in part-time, paid employment in community agencies and community service jobs. The Job Training Partnership Act includes special initiatives for employment of older workers in full- and part-time jobs in the community. Additional opportunities for older worker employment through federal programs include the Teacher Corps, which provides experienced teachers to assist disadvantaged children; Adult Basic Education programs in public schools and colleges, which use volunteers as teacher aides; the Bureau of the Census, which trains older (and other) persons as interviewers; and the Veterans Administration, which trains and uses volunteers in a variety of activities.

Retirees who are interested in any of these programs can get information from their local senior center, area agency on aging, state unit on aging, or information and referral program. Additional employment opportunities for older persons are discussed below.

Competitive Employment

Retirees can compete in the labor market for any and all jobs. The Age Discrimination in Employment Act (P. L. 90-202) prohibits employers from discriminating in employee selection on the basis of age criteria for persons aged 40–70. Since there is no upper age limit for federal employment, older persons can seek federal jobs through the U.S. Civil Service Commission, which has more than 70 centers throughout the country. The United States Employment Services Offices are required to designate one counselor per office to specialize in job placement of older workers. Retirees can receive free employment counseling and also vocational testing at their state employment office. Many communities have a special nonprofit older worker employment agency that will provide free or low-cost testing and counseling. Other have special vocational counseling, training, and/or job placement programs for older workers through community colleges.

Jobs in the competitive labor market can be located in numerous ways. These include public and private employment agencies, newspaper ads, yellow pages of telephone books, and labor unions. Service organizations such as the Salvation Army, YMCA, and Jewish centers can be sources of job information. Although each source can be helpful, it is important to remember that 85% or more of jobs are obtained by word of mouth. Hence, retirees seeking employment will benefit from making their needs known to friends and family members as well as agency staff. Obtaining jobs in the competitive labor market can be difficult, for reasons discussed below.

Barriers to Labor Force Participation for Older Workers

Negative attitudes toward older persons in our society include stereotypes that keep employers from hiring older workers. These stereotypes, or myths, are similar to those that affect employment of handicapped persons (22, 23. The following are several prominent myths that have proved to be untrue in multiple research studies: (a) Older persons cannot meet the physical demands of jobs; (b) older workers are slow and cannot meet production requirements; (c) older workers have poor attendance records; (d) older workers are inflexible; and (e) intellectual ability declines with age. The truth about these myths is as follows: (a) Less than 14% of jobs require any great physical strength; (b) there is no significant drop in productivity with age; (c) older workers have good attendance records; (d) many older persons are very adaptable, and this quality is related to individual personality factors and not to age; and (e) intelligence does not decline with age. Older persons learn as well as persons of younger ages, when changes in reaction time are considered and new materials are presented at a slightly slower pace.

Older workers face barriers to employment relating to the Social Security ceiling on earnings and may find that part-time employment best suits their needs for continuing incomes. Special provisions of Social Security, Supplemental Security Income, and pension plans may affect decisions on continuing employment for some retirees. Since these change over time, older workers should consult their local Social Security office or pension plan representative to determine current policies or ceilings on earnings.

Self-Employment

Self-employment is also an option for retirees. The possibilities are virtually limitless and include homebound employment as well as the operation of businesses elsewhere in the community. Self-employment can, but does not necessarily, allow flexibility in time schedules and work priorities. Services to the community, small businesses, and so forth must maintain regular hours in order to promote repeat business. Many self-employment options allow great flexibility in time schedules, which is desirable for certain retirees. The flexibility in time permits various lifestyle adjustments, including attention to leisure and recreation needs.

Self-employment is not without risks. Typically, some investment of funds is required to initiate a business. Since many small businesses fail, older persons electing this option may benefit from contact with the local office of the U. S. Small Business Administration. The Small Business Administration lends seed money to assist in the development of small businesses and also lends consultive expertise through SCORE (discussed earlier) and other programs. Self-employment can restrict time available for vacations, travel, and other leisure pursuits, as well as provide income for those activities.

ALLOCATING BLOCKS OF TIME FOR LEISURE

Leisure often is defined in opposition to work. Time that is not work time or preparation for work time is leisure or free time. It is time for which one chooses one's activities (24). Choices of leisure-time activities are made according to values and attitudes toward work and leisure (25). The cessation of the work role at the time of retirement creates a sudden increase in leisure time (1, 26). Whether or not retirees choose to continue working, some attention to the use of free time will enhance life satisfaction during the retirement years (2).

Leisure activities can provide an alternate means for achieving status and can help the retiree to meet needs previously satisfied by work. Satisfying leisure-time activities can contribute to an increased sense of well-being and enhance self-esteem. Some planning for effective use of leisure time can be helpful for most older persons, though some prefer and enjoy a total lack of structure for their time. Planning for leisure time ideally will begin prior to retirement, though planning at any time should result in positive outcomes (27, 28).

Harris and Associates (18), as part of a major national study, examined activities of a representative sample of older persons. They rank ordered 15 common activities and noted the percentage of older persons engaging in each. The top-ranked activities, in descending order of preference, were socializing with friends (47%), reading (36%), watching television (36%), caring for younger or older family members (27%), participating in recreational activities or hobbies (26%), and taking walks, jogging, or other exercise (25%). The least popular activities of older persons reported in an earlier survey (29) were just doing nothing (15%), working full or part time (10%), doing volunteer work (8%), taking part in political activities (14%), and participating in sports (golf, tennis, etc.) (15%).

The data from the Harris and Associates studies support the diversity among older persons. It is impossible to suggest certain activities for such a diverse group. Rather, it is important to stress to retirees the need for planning use of leisure time to meet their individual needs. Some, as noted above, prefer a total lack of structure. Others prefer structure at some times and/or in some areas, but not in others. For example, some retirees choose to participate in travel groups or local service programs, while others select living environments that include social and recreation directors and ongoing, varied programs.

Structuring use of one's leisure time in some manner can be an effective means of time management. Moreover, the structure and activities chosen can contribute to a sense of purposefulness and meaning for retirees. Leisure activities present opportunities for socialization and interactions with persons of all ages.

Financial considerations are an important part of leisure planning. Numerous public programs, such as the National Park Service, offer free or reduced rates for older persons. Services through the Older Americans Act provide low or no-cost leisure programs as well. In addition, the latter programs are structured to provide opportunities for socialization with others. Many community and civic organizations sponsor leisure programs for older persons, through clubs, special events, and other activities.

Leisure activities are chosen primarily on the basis of interest, though amount of time, income, and availability of leisure partners are important parameters affecting individual choices (30). Lifelong hobbies and free-time activities may continue in retirement, often with more time devoted to those that have proved to be enjoyable. New activities may be chosen as a result of finally having the free time to experiment. Retirees or preretirees considering leisure choices or options for planning use of leisure time may benefit from use of leisure interest inventories to encourage exploration of their options (30).

Attitudes toward leisure tend to be fairly consistent over time. Persons who have not developed leisure pursuits during their working years may have difficulty adjusting to the increased free time and leisure opportunities presented by retirement (31), unless they overcome or reinterpret the meaning of work and leisure. Bosse and Ekerdt (32) suggested that adoption of "the busy ethic" could provide moral continuity between work and retirement and facilitate the transition to increased leisure. The problem encountered by many retirees usually is not a lack of available opportunities, but rather a lack of experience in "leisuring." Just as people learn to choose an occupation, choice of leisure pursuits can be learned. One activity that increasing numbers of retirees are choosing to help meet their leisure needs is education, which can be a source of information as well as an effective use of time in and of itself.

ORGANIZING A LEARNING PROGRAM

Those retirees who want to continue learning have abundant opportunities to do so (18). Reasons for continuing formal education include attaining new skills, enhancing and sharpening old skills, exploring new areas of interest, exploring areas of interest postponed in earlier years because of other commitments, and simply learning new and different subjects and methods.

Sources of continuing education include public adult education program, community colleges, vocational and technical school activities, and college and university courses. Many of these education programs have reduced or no fees for older persons. One special worldwide program, Elderhostel, provides for reduced fees for older persons to live on college campuses and participate in course work, usually during certain weeks of summer sessions but also during the academic year. Courses need not be part of a degree program, but can be taken simply for their intrinsic interest.

Course work may be didactic, experiential, or both. It can involve academic subject matter, crafts, technology, or some combination. Community college courses are available for learning everything from computer programming to belly dancing. Instructors from these programs frequently offer courses through local senior centers; thus participants who desire course work with age peers are assured of having this need met.

The number of older persons taking advantage of education programs is increasing. In 1974, only 2% of older people were enrolled in educational courses (29), compared with 5% in 1988 (28). These courses are taken mainly at colleges (27%), community and senior centers (24%), places of business (18%), adult education schools (12%), and churches (6%). The reasons given by older persons for taking courses are to acquire job skills (74%), to expand general knowledge about some field or hobby (63%), to make good use of one's time (18%), and to be with other people (4%).

The only limitations to education are set by the needs and interests of the retiree. It is possible to go overboard and sign up for more courses than one has the time or energy to complete. Again, planning is the key to an effective learning program. Effective planning requires adequate information; therefore, the retiree's first step is to obtain catalogs and other information from all local educational programs. The senior center, information and referral agency, and area agency on aging are ready sources of information on available programs in the community. Things to consider include costs, when and where courses are offered, course requirements, transportation and parking arrangements, and intrinsic interest. Course sequences can be planned, or courses can be taken one at a time when an attractive course is offered.

One of the problems faced by learning programs is the motivation of older persons to learn. The all too common belief is that education is for younger people; certainly, schools are associated with youth, not with older adults. A typical point of view was expressed by one man when advised to consider taking career preparation courses at a local community college: "But, I'm fifty years old!"

Some of the barriers to adult learning have been listed by Cross (30). The first type is *situational,* which arises at particular times in one's life such as costs, no transportation, home or job responsibilities, or geographical isolation. The second is *dispositional,* which includes negative attitudes toward learning activities or oneself as a learner. The third is *institutional,* which refers to inconvenient scheduling of classes, amount of fee structure, or restrictive locations of classes.

One of the possible answers to this problem of motivation may be found when individuals experience a life change in connection with a career shift, a developing interest in some leisure activity, or added family responsibilities. Any of these changes or related changes are likely to create needs for individuals to undertake behaviors that they find unfamiliar and/or difficult. As a result, they can be motivated to learn new information and new skills that will enable them to be more effective in the new situation. A necessary element here is information regarding the availability of learning programs.

Planning an educational program can be an enjoyable part of planning a total leisure lifestyle. Counseling, both individual and group, to assist retirees in their planning is available through both community colleges and universities. A major area to consider when planning is balance of activities to enhance life satisfaction and enjoyment.

STRIVING FOR A REASONABLE BALANCE

Within the counseling and psychology professions, major theorists consistently have encouraged persons to work toward balanced lives in order to achieve and maintain psychological health. For Freud, the balance was to be achieved between the three major life tasks of work, love, and play. Adler suggested the need to balance the three tasks of work, love, and friendship. Overemphasis in any one area, an unbalanced life, can lead to unhappiness and low self-esteem, thus inhibiting life satisfaction.

Achieving balance is a process, not an event. Life itself is a process; it occurs over time. Therefore, achieving balance in the major tasks of life also must occur over time. It is a process of trial and error, with one or the other component taking precedence at different times depending on needs in an individual's life (27).

The point has been made that planning is important for successful adjustment to retirement. Consideration of balance is an essential component of planning. The retired years offer the greatest opportunity of life for practicing time management. It is also a challenge, a challenge to create a life that is pleasant and enjoyable, and meets one's needs for growth and development in the later years. Many people, unused to such a situation, can benefit from counseling interventions to help them make the most of their time during retirement.

IMPLICATIONS FOR COUNSELORS

A number of implications for counselors are suggested by the information in this chapter. Counselors have a vital role to play in helping retirees plan effective and satisfying uses of their time during retirement. Some attention to values clarification and setting of priorities typically will be required (19, 34).

The salience of the work role in the lives of most persons virtually necessitates some attention to personal interpretations of work in the counseling setting. Counselors can help retirees examine their attitudes and values concerning work and the needs that work meets in their lives. This information can help retirees make a decision of whether to continue working. If not, the same information forms the basis for selection of leisure activities to help meet the needs formerly met through work activities. Clarification of lifestyle choices, including location and type of housing environment, social needs, and so forth are important components of the values clarification process.

Counselor's repertoires of information should include employment opportunities and knowledge of community agencies to assist older workers in locating employment. Counselors will benefit from some awareness of labor market trends in order to help retirees plan a late-life career that may span several or many years.

Another important area for exploration is the retiree's attitudes and values about leisure. Many of today's older persons were encouraged to work rather than "to leisure" for most of their lives. Now they may place a low priority on leisure activities. Counselors can help older persons to reexamine and to reconsider their priorities for leisure activities. Leisure counseling may be preventive, remedial, or both, helping retirees to reexamine existing activities as well as develop new activities to meet their needs. The assistance of counselors in planning educational programs, and providing information about various courses and resources, will be important for many retired persons.

Loesch (35) proposed a seven-step model for leisure counseling with older persons that presents a useful strategy for counselors. The steps are implemented in sequence as follows:

1 Determination of the need for counseling, using both formal and informal assessments;

2 Evaluation of current leisure satisfaction to determine if there is a need for counseling in relation to leisure;

3 Determination of an appropriate counseling orientation or method;

4 Comprehensive evaluation of the person in all life arenas;

5 Determination of whether the goal of counseling is to identify and/or select leisure pursuits that will contribute to life satisfaction, improved self-concept, or some other desired change;

6 Determination of the most appropriate leisure activities for the older person;

7 Evaluation of the process.

The last step can lead to reentry into the process at any of the preceding six steps.

The use of inventories to assess leisure preference, styles, and attitudes is a useful adjunct to counseling with retirees. McDowell and Clark (31) reviewed several currently available inventories which could be used with older persons. In addition, Overs, Taylor, Cassell, and Chennor (36) developed leisure activities blanks that are readily available and useful. Vocational interest inventories used in counseling with persons of other age groups can be helpful to older persons in choosing both work and leisure activities.

Helping retirees determine effective strategies for time management can be very much a part of the counseling process. The need for balance is important, and represents one of the essential areas for exploration. Counselors can facilitate discussion of attitudes, values, and lifestyles in relation to work, love, and friendship, and all of the life arenas discussed earlier. Identification of areas for change and/or further development can be facilitated through the counseling process.

GROUP ACTIVITIES

I Assume for a moment that your life is your job. Write a job description for yourself. The description may be written in two parts:

    A Divide a paper into five columns. Write your assets in terms of education, employment experiences, hobbies, interpersonal relationship skills, and other personal qualities in the five columns, respectively.

    B Write a position description for yourself, assuming life to be the position. Include the following at a minimum: (a) brief general description of job (your life); (b) specific duties of your life, with approximate amount of time devoted to each; and (c) necessary and desirable characteristics for fulfillment of the job requirements. Remember that you have 24 hr per day in life, 7 days per week, and 365 days per year. Your job description should "keep you busy" the full time.

How do your assets match up with the requirements of your job? Are there areas you would like to change? In what ways? Discuss your job/life description in groups of three to five persons. Discuss group reactions in the full group at the end of the activity.

II   Obtain copies of one or more leisure interest inventories. Fill them out, score, and discuss in groups of two or more.

REFERENCES

1   Havighurst, R. J. (1961). The nature and values of meaningful free-time activity. In R. J. Kleemeier (Ed.), *Aging and leisure* (pp. 338–343). New York: Oxford University Press.

2   Myers, J. E. (1984). Leisure counseling for older people. In E. T. Dowd (Ed.), *Leisure counseling: Concepts and applications* (pp. 157–177). Springfield, IL: Charles C. Thomas.

3   Iso-Ahola, S. E. (1980). *Social psychological perspectives on retirement and leisure.* Springfield, IL: Charles C. Thomas.

4   Tolbert, E. L. (1980). *Counseling for career development* (2nd ed.). Boston, MA: Houghton-Mifflin.

5   Super, D. (1957). *The psychology of careers.* New York: Harper and Brothers.

6   Van Hoose, W. H., & Worth, M. R. (1982). *Adulthood in the life cycle.* Dubuque, IA: William C. Brown.

7   Palmore, E. (1973). Predicting longevity. In *Work in America* (pp. xxx–xxx). Washington, DC: Department of Health, Education and Welfare.

8   Super, D. (1977). Vocational maturity in mid-career. *Vocational Guidance Quarterly, 25,* 294–303.

9   Super, D. (1980). A life-span, life space approach to career development. *Journal of Vocational Behavior, 16,* 282–298.

10 Kimmel, D. C. (1975). *Adulthood and aging.* New York: Wiley.

11 Atchley, R. C. (1977). *The social forces in later life.* Belmont, CA: Wadsworth.

12 Czaka, S. J. (1986, February). Retraining middle-aged and older workers. Presented at the Invitational Conference on Work, Aging, and Visual Impairment. Washington, DC.

13 Kieffer, J. A. (1980). Counselors and the older worker: An overview. *Journal of Employment Counseling, 17*(1), 8–16.

14 Rosen, B., & Jender, T. H. (1985). *Older employees: New roles for valued resources.* Homewood, IL: Dow-Jones-Irwin.

15 Barocas, V., & Morrison, M. (1985). Employee, retiree options for an aging work force. *Business and Health, 2*(5), 25–29.

16 Blyton, P. (1984). Older workers, retirement and the need for flexibility. *Employee Relations, 6*(2), 1–11.

17 Burr, E. W. (1986). What next after 50? *Journal of Counseling and Development 13*(2), 23–29.

18 Harris, L., & Associates. (1984). *Aging in the eighties: America in transition.* Washington, DC: National Council on the Aging.

19 Miletti, M. A. (1984). *Voices of experience: 1500 retired people talk about retirement.* New York: Teachers Insurance and Annuity Association, College Retirement Equity Fund.

20 Administration on Aging. (1976). *Employment and volunteer opportunities for older people* (DHHS Publication No. 76-20233). Washington, DC: U.S. Government Printing Office.

21 Action for Independent Maturity, (1978). *AIMs guide to the time in your life.* Washington, DC: American Association of Retired Persons.

22 Myers, J. E. (1981). Counseling the disabled older person for the world of work. *Journal of Employment Counseling, 17*(1), 37–48.

23 Mitchell, K. (1987). The aging workforce and the politics of incapacity. In L. G. Perlman & G. F. Austin (Eds.), *The aging workforce: Implications for rehabilitation* (pp. 17–25). Alexandria, VA: National Rehabilitation Association.

24 Kleemeier, R. W. (Ed.). (1961). *Aging and leisure: A research perspective into the meaningful use of time.* New York: Oxford University Press.

25 McEvoy, L. H. (1979). The leisure preferences, problems, and needs of the elderly. *Journal of Leisure Research, 11*(1). 40–47.

26 McDaniel, C. (1977). Leisure and career development at mid-life; A rationale. *Vocational Guidance Quarterly, 24,* 344–350.

27 Bolles, R. (1978). *The three boxes of life.* Berkeley, CA: Ten Speed Press.

28 McDaniels, C. (1982). *Leisure: Integrating a neglected component in life planning.* Columbus, OH: National Center for Research in Vocational Education.

29 Harris, L., & Associates. (1974). *The myth and reality of aging in America.* Washington, DC: National Council on the Aging.

30 Cross, K. P. (1981). *Adults as learners.* San Francisco: Jossey-Bass.

31 McDowell, C. F., & Clark, P. (1982). Assessing the leisure needs of older persons. *Measurement and Evaluation in Counseling and Guidance, 15*(2), 228–239.

32 Bosse, R., & Ekerdt, D. J. (1981). Change in self-perception of leisure activities with retirement. *Gerontologist, 21*(6), 650–654.

33 Ekerdt, D. J. (1986). The busy ethic: Moral continuity between work and retirement. *Gerontologist, 26*(3), 293–294.

34 McDowell, C. F. (1981). Leisure: Consciousness, well being, and counseling. *Counseling Psychologist, 9*(3), 3–32.

35 Loesch, L. C. (1981). Leisure counseling for disabled older persons. *Journal of Rehabilitation, 47*(4), 58–63.

36 Overs, A., Taylor, C., Cassell, B., & Chennor, R. (1977). *A vocational counseling for the elderly.* Washington, DC: Office of Human Development.

APPENDIX: Leisure Interest Inventories

Constructive Leisure Activity Survey (CLAS): A comprehensive inventory consisting of over 300 items in which respondents indicate past and future leisure likes and dislikes. See Edwards, P. B. (1979). *Leisure counseling techniques: Individual and group counseling step-by-step.* Los Angeles, CA: University Publishers.

Leisure Activities Blank (LAB): The most standardized instrument in the field of leisure wellness, this 120-item inventory measures past and future leisure involvements. Past interest subscales are mechanics, crafts, intellectual, slow living, sports, and glamour sports. Future interest subscales include adventure, mechanics, crafts, easy living, intellectual, ego recognition, slow living, and clean living. See Mc-Kechnie, G. E. (1974). *The Leisure Activities Blank Manual.* Palo Alto, CA: Consulting Psychologists Press.

Leisure Well-Being Inventory (LWBI): 125 yes–no items survey the subject's breadth of leisure wellness. This instrument has been widely used and researched because it goes beyond measuring simple leisure interests and assesses four aspects: coping, awareness–understanding, knowledge, and assertion. See McDowell, C. F. (1978). *Leisure Well-Being Inventory.* Eugene, OR: Leisure Lifestyle Consultants.

Mirenda Leisure Interest Finder (MLIF): Using the column format for checking off leisure interests and needs, this 90-item instrument has been computerized and widely used for assessing leisure interests. The items were selected from the nine categories of leisure activities on the Avocational Activities Inventory. See Wilson, G. T., & Mirenda, J. J. (1975). The Milwaukee Leisure Counseling Model. *Counseling and Values, 20,* 42–46.

Chapter Eight

Deciding on a Place to Live

A common question among older persons who are considering retirement is "Where shall we live?" This question arises for several reasons. In the first place, their family composition has changed, with the departure of the younger members. The interests and needs of the older members have also changed, with their retirement from full-time employment. Still the family residence remains as a symbol of a vital social grouping that, in the eyes of many older adults, should be maintained. It provides feelings of independence, continuity, and stability so important in a changing world.

As of 1983, 75% of the total households headed by older persons in the United States were owner occupied (1, p. 116). The remaining 25% were rental units. As married couples and single women grow older, they tend to live in rental housing. Older single men, however, are somewhat more likely to own their own homes (1). Older persons often live in older homes, whether they own or rent them. As of 1980, more of those persons age 65 or older were recorded as living in the suburbs rather than in the central cities.

The living conditions were reported to be unsatisfactory in slightly more than 10% of the housing units occupied by older persons in 1983. In those units there was evidence of mice and rats. In about 9%, there were bedrooms that did not provide privacy, that is, open holes and cracks could be seen in these units, and, in lesser numbers, plumbing and kitchen facilities were incomplete. In the case of rental units, about 15% of the older men and nearly 7% of the older women did not have telephones, an important means of communication, especially for older persons (1).

Generally, rates of moving tend to decline as persons grow older. During the 1970s, the number jumped by 50% over the number who moved during the 1960s. In the 1982–1983 period about 5% of all older persons moved. The greatest percentage moved from one site to another, with almost half migrating to Florida, California, Arizona, Texas, and New Jersey. During the past two decades, more than 25% of the total moved to Florida. Those who moved were generally well educated, financially well off, and usually joined by a spouse. Of those who moved to the Sunbelt in the early part of their retirement, a relatively small number eventually returned to their home states to be near their adult children (2).

In times past, the alternatives were few for those who wanted to move. Today, the alternatives are many and depend on individual economic resources, as well as personal preferences. The housing industry in this country has discovered that retirement housing is one of the mushrooming markets and has developed a number of options offering a variety of services and lifestyles.

This chapter focuses on the question, Where shall other persons live after retirement? Reasons for continuing to live in the family home or for moving elsewhere are considered. Those choosing to move should explore the quality of the environment at the location under investigation. This exploration should include the social and the physical environment, the first from the point of view of congeniality and accessibility, and the second in terms of adaptability to the individual's changing needs. Various housing options for independent older persons, as well as options for semidependent and dependent older persons are reviewed. Some of the current housing issues are summarized, including the need for information, the importance of maintaining an independent lifestyle, and the affordability factor. The implications for counselors of the housing question and its varied solutions are presented, and group activities are listed to emphasize the importance of housing in meeting the special needs of older persons.

REASONS FOR STAYING OR MOVING

Older persons often value their homes as places to live. These homes have been built or remodeled just as the owners wanted them and furnished in the same way. They have adequate space with rooms for visiting children, grandchildren, and friends to spend the night. The chances are that shopping facilities are readily available. The neighbors are congenial and the neighborhood is satisfactory. The mortgage has been paid for, so there is no rent. These are some of the reasons why older persons like to stay in their family homes.

There are also valid reasons why older persons want to move. Their homes now have too much space. They are difficult to clean and to maintain. Often they are in need of modifications to accommodate those older persons who are experiencing some physical disabilities. The neighborhood may be changing; long-time friends and neighbors may have moved away. The adult children have moved to other states and can visit only occasionally. Shopping facilities are no longer conveniently available. Taxes and the cost of utilities and repairs go up every year. Tax laws make it possible to exempt from the sale of the family residence $125,000 which can be applied to a small house in another location. The advantages of moving to one of the Sunbelt states include warmer weather and lower costs for winter heating and clothing. Changes in lifestyles, which make more leisure time available, sometimes make it both appropriate and desirable to change place of residence.

In 1986, a nationwide survey was made for the American Association of Retired Persons of housing occupied by older persons over 60 years of age. This survey sampled housing needs, concerns, and preferences. In general, those surveyed indicated a high degree of satisfaction with their housing and the communities within which they lived. The elements given most favorable ratings were location, comfort, the neighborhood, size of residence or property, and no steps. Elements rated most unfavorable were number of steps, indoor maintenance, location, including absence of public transportation, lack of efficiency, outdoor maintenance, and cost of utilities (3).

Older persons deciding to move have very important decisions to make. Leaving the family home means finding another home that meets the criteria of comfort, conveniences, less space (but enough to accommodate furnishings being brought from the family home), a congenial neighborhood, and available transportation and shopping facilities. The new community should offer educational, social, and cultural activities.

The first step in the process of deciding to move is to select the state. The second is to visit different sections of the state, perhaps living in different locations for a winter or a summer season. The third step is to locate and decide on a particular residence—the new family home. This residence may be a separate house, a mobile home, a rented apartment, a condominium, or a cooperative housing unit. It may be located in the central part of the city, a suburb, or a rural area. It may be part of a retirement community.

Retirees are especially interested in places to live that provide security and financial peace of mind. Their choice of a place to live is finally determined by cost.

QUALITY OF ENVIRONMENT

Of great importance is the environment within which the housing unit is located and which it helps to create. This environment is both physical and social.

The physical element consists of bricks and mortar, all the materials of which the physical element is made. It includes the amount and arrangement of space, both outside and inside the unit being evaluated. The materials should be durable, easy to maintain, pleasing to the eye, and comfortable to the touch. Location and size of doors and windows can be significant: Doors need to provide ease of physical access and facilitate social communication with neighbors; windows need to open to natural beauty out of doors, bringing the outside inside, and enable the resident to see human activities of interest including pedestrians passing by. The placement of exterior doors in adjacent housing units may help or hinder the development of acquaintance patterns among neighbors.

The amount and arrangement of physical space within the housing unit can do much to influence the feelings of older residents about living there. The sense of openness can be achieved by the size of the windows, mirrors, limited partition walls, and the use of colors in wall paint and furnishings. The sense of security can be aided by using larger locks for doors and windows, providing nonskid floor materials, and installing electronic systems to deter the entry of thieves and to make emergency contact with medical personnel.

The Social Element

The social element of the environment is made up of the people with whom older persons come in contact. These people are members of the family, associates in the workplace, and neighbors or others in the community; some are known through religious or civic groups with which the older persons are affiliated. With each of these individuals or groups the older person takes a role and exerts influence or is influenced in attitudes and behaviors. For example, if associates in the workplace have negative attitudes toward retirement, then the older person tends to have negative attitudes also.

Older persons demonstrate a wide range of reactions to the social environment as they age. Some withdraw from their activities and associations with other people. The theory is that this withdrawal is mutual on the part of older persons and the people who make up their social environment. Other older persons continue their life patterns of involvement in a variety of activities that give them personal satisfaction. Carp has provided some evidence that positive environmental conditions tend to produce an involvement in activities rather than withdrawal from life (4). The activity theory suggests that older persons keep active as long as possible and that replacements should be selected when customary activities can no longer be maintained. The point is that an active rather than a passive approach to life appears to be conducive to mental health and satisfaction (5).

Carp has emphasized that housing for older persons should be understood as much more than physical structure; it should be seen as a total environment embracing every part of living (4). This environment should address the needs of older persons; it should facilitate meaningful life experiences and encourage older persons' development as useful citizens of their communities.

Aside from the people, the elements of this environment include the age and ownership of the housing units, their physical condition and maintenance level, their location in terms of services (shopping, banking, medical facilities, churches, synagogues, recreational facilities), adequacy of transportation, availability of peers and relatives, and the nature of the surrounding neighborhood, both physical and social (6). The quality of the housing environment might be evaluated in terms of these various elements listed by Carp, particularly as their totality affects the individual's life experiences and positive growth. Thus the all-important feature of the housing environment is the people who will live there, and their needs.

Aging in Place

An important concept to be considered in the planning and selection of housing for older persons is that they should have the opportunity for *aging in place.* This concept has three major assumptions: First, the physical capabilities of people change as thy age; second, their interests in and capabilities for social relationships and activities change; and third, they should have every opportunity to maintain an independent lifestyle for as long as possible. Each of these assumptions requires that planners and family members, including the older persons themselves, consider the following questions as they decide on a place to live:

1 Can the physical facilities under consideration, either new construction or older family dwellings, be modified over time to met the changing needs of older persons whose physical capabilities can be expected to decrease over time? For example, should interior and exterior doors be equipped with levers rather than knobs for hands affected by arthritis? Should storage spaces be arranged within easy access reach to avoid the use of ladders or chairs?

2 Are senior centers, churches, synagogues, and recreation clubs readily accessible to provide opportunities for new social relationships and for activities to meet changing interests?

3 Are there available in the community services that will enable older persons to maintain extended independent lifestyles while living in their homes? Such services might include home-delivered meals; homemakers to assist with cleaning, shopping, dressing, and possibly food preparation; volunteer services to assist with minor home maintenance; or home nursing care.

Financial assistance for older persons to maintain independent housing is now provided by some state governments in the form of a reduction in property taxes. In Florida, for example, homestead exemption legislation has removed from the tax rolls homesteads with an assessed value of $25,000 or less. Taxes are collected on homesteads valued at more than $25,000. Some municipalities, or power companies, have programs that assist older persons with their utility bills. Also in Florida, a Community Care for the Elderly Program, funded by the state, focuses essential community services on frail elderly through a case management system. For this state, this program is much less costly than providing support in nursing homes.

In the United States, there has been a tendency to plan for some form of institutional housing for older persons who require assistance with their daily living requirements. Through providing essential services in their homes, state or local governments or agencies can make it possible for older persons experiencing physical limitations to remain independent for longer times within their own homes. The advantages are both financial and personal, in the sense of helping older persons to maintain relatively independent lifestyles.

HOUSING OPTIONS FOR INDEPENDENT OLDER PERSONS

What, then, are the options available to older persons who can and prefer to live independently? These options, which are discussed below, include remaining in the family, home, remodeling for an accessory apartment, renting an apartment, purchasing a smaller home, purchasing a mobile manufactured home, buying a condominium or a cooperative housing unit, joining a retirement community, living with adult children in Elder Cottage Housing Opportunity (ECHO) housing, or arranging for shared housing.

Remaining in the Family Home

Some of the advantages and disadvantages of remaining in the family home are listed in the beginning of this chapter. A major advantage is that the home may be paid for, making possible maximum personal independence, financial freedom, and comfort. A large disadvantage may be building and grounds maintenance. The big questions to be answered are "What is my lifestyle now, and what lifestyle do I want to have during my retirement?" Answers to these questions are important in deciding among the housing options.

Remodeling for Accessory Apartment

If the family home is sizable and there is much space unneeded by the older family member, the decision may be to remodel part of the home into an accessory apartment for rent which will be a completely private, separated living unit. This decision is likely to be based on one or more of the following situations: The older person needs some additional income; he or she needs a greater sense of security, including the availability of someone living in proximity to provide a feeling of companionship; and the older person wants relief from the burdens of excess spaces to be cleaned, heated, and maintained. The occupant of the accessory unit could expect some reduction in rent for services provided to the owner.

An accessory apartment located in the homes of adult children may be the best answer for older persons who need to be near their children, but want to retain their own independence.

ECHO Housing

If space for an accessory apartment is not available in the homes of adult children, an alternative is ECHO housing. This type of housing is manufactured, portable, and located on the property of adult children. It meets the need for proximity to family members while preserving the mutual needs for personal independence.

This type of housing was started in Australia where it was known as "granny flats." It has been authorized in several counties of at least three states (California, Arizona, and Pennsylvania) as an exception to single-family zoning. However, it is likely to arouse strong opposition from property owners in residential neighborhoods who are fearful of any modification of zoning restrictions. Where ECHO housing units have been installed, both the older persons and adult children have praised the results.

Owning a Home

If personal independence is an important factor, purchasing a new home may be the best option. Cost considerations, however, must be carefully evaluated. On the one hand, using the proceeds from the sale of the family home has real advantages, since the proceeds, up to $125,000, are exempt from federal income tax. On the other hand, all of the costs involved in the purchase must be considered, including the closing costs, special city or county assessments, insurance, property taxes, utilities and trash collection, furnishings, interior decoration, and landscaping.

Location is also an important factor. Purchase prices of homes vary considerably by geographical region of the country. New housing developments are often located at some distance from the town or city. The impact of travel distances for services on living in such locations must be considered.

When a new home is being contemplated, one of the options is selecting a two-family dwelling, or duplex, with the anticipated advantage of gaining some rental income to help finance the purchase. A problem with this option is the management responsibility, which includes maintenance, repairs, and obtaining renters who are sympathetic to the older adults' lifestyle.

Purchasing a Mobile Manufactured Home

More and more people are purchasing mobile manufactured homes because they are less expensive, more efficient, and constructed under quality controls. Construction standards have been set by the U.S. Department of Housing and Urban Development. Purchase covers furniture and equipment. The amount of space in the larger homes is surprising. Special features may include a carport, porch, and greenhouse windows.

These homes are being used by many cooperatives and condominiums in retirement communities. A potential problem in some situations is the sale of the property to new owners who may wish to resell the land for other purposes. Therefore, it is important to examine in detail the terms under which the manufactured home and its site are purchased or rented.

Living in a Condominium or Cooperative

In a condominium, individuals purchase and own their own living units which are part of a group of housing units. The common-use facilities are jointly owned with all other unit owners. The condominium's business and activities are managed by an elected board of directors who may select a management organization to operate the condominium.

A cooperative is similar, with the significant difference that it is a nonprofit organization that owns and operates the total housing project for all members. Individuals purchase shares in the cooperative and thereby are entitled to occupy their particular units and use the common-use facilities; they are responsible for the overall ownership and management of the cooperative. They elect a governing board to provide the management functions.

In both types of housing, older persons have the advantages of freedom from maintenance responsibilities and opportunities for social interaction and participation. However, when buying a unit in a condominium, purchasers must carefully read the "condominium declaration" and the "condominium by-laws" to understand what obligations they are assuming, such as fees, and the limitations on the use of their living unit.

In terms of tax benefits, condominiums have similar advantages to owning a home. A possible difficulty with cooperatives is the way in which the value of an individual's shares is determined. This value can be frozen at the price paid for the shares when the individual moved in. It can be established on the basis of original price plus the property's appreciation. It can be set by the current market, benefiting from the general rise in values of similar properties. In a financial sense, there are some differences between a condominium and a cooperative. For example, property taxes may be less in a cooperative, and cooperatives may be eligible for some federal and local subsidy programs.

Retirement Communities

Retirement communities are generally self-contained and limited to older persons who have retired from full-time work. Age restrictions are often set at a minimum of 50 years, although some retirement communities have none, so that a number of residents may not be either retired or older.

As of 1984, the number of retirement communities in the United States was estimated at 2,300, providing housing for almost one million persons, located especially in Florida, Arizona, and California (7). In terms of housing types, more than half are apartment units, 15% are mobile homes, and fewer than 2% are single-family dwellings.

Retirement communities often provide a wide range of services to meet a variety of interests and preferences. Minimum services include trash collection, yard care, and common-use facilities for social and recreational activities. Some communities focus on special interests. For example, the College Harbor community located on the campus of Eckerd College in St. Petersburg, Florida, stresses scholarly interests; the Fairbanks Ranch, near San Diego, California, emphasizes sports. Other communities target particular types of retirees such as former secretaries at Vista Grande in Rio Rancho, New Mexico, and Asian retirees at Heiwas Terrace in Chicago, Illinois (8).

Many older persons are looking for a new living environment to provide association with persons of similar interests, a stimulating program of activities, a sense of security, and peace of mind. They can find these qualities in some retirement communities, but they must search for the particular one which fulfills their requirements.

Selection is limited by costs and the funds available to the retiree. Of course, costs are determined by both the quality of the housing unit and by the services and activities provided. The basic cost is for the housing unit itself. In addition, there is a monthly fee to cover services, such as grounds upkeep. Sometimes there are separate fees for meals and activities. Individuals looking at a retirement community should obtain a list of the various costs and fees and examine the contract carefully to learn what cost increases may occur in the future.

Some concerns are expressed about certain features of retirement communities, such as the value of separating older persons from younger persons and whether there are too many (or too few) activities. Answers to these concerns depend on the lifestyle preference of the individual. The indications are that, by and large, residents of such communities agree with the age requirements and experience a great deal of involvement, personal commitment to the community, and general satisfaction.

Renting a House or Apartment

Rentals have the virtue of releasing older persons from most property responsibilities, such as property taxes, building upkeep and repairs, and grounds maintenance. The rental unit and equipment may be more compact, with less space available than in the family home. At the same time, more services are usually provided. In comparing rental versus purchase of a home, older persons should remember that the payment of rent does not build up equity in the property.

Shared Housing

Shared housing also known as Co-operative Housing, can be an economical means for older persons to obtain comfortable, adequate housing. Usually a public or private agency purchases older but larger private residences. Two or more unrelated individuals occupy their own private rooms and share the common-use spaces.

They may also share responsibility for housekeeping, maintenance, financing, management, and selection of new or replacement residents. Performance of such functions as these by the older person can be regarded as contributions toward rent determined by costs. Another arrangement involves payment of a specified rent depending on the tasks assigned to the residents. In either case, a cook is usually employed to handle food preparation.

In addition to being an economical option, shared housing has the advantage of providing companionship, security, and involvement in a mutual enterprise that contributes to a sense of self-worth. A possible disadvantage is the necessity of getting along with others in the house.

Another form of shared housing is the large home that the older owner wishes to share with another person or persons of compatible age. Such persons help with running the house or pay rent to hire the housework to be done. Often, private agencies assist with "matching" older persons together. A variation of this arrangement is the "matching" of an older person with a younger person who assists the older homeowner with personal needs.

A major problem may be financing of shared housing by potential sponsors. Providing this form of housing for low-income older persons ordinarily requires the combined efforts of the public and private sectors. Obtaining funds for acquiring properties for shared housing is part of the problem; another part is overcoming zoning restrictions on suitable properties, which are usually located in residential neighborhoods. However, the sharing of their homes on an informal basis by older persons has increased considerably during the 1970s, by as much as 35%. According to more recent census data more than 600,000 persons over 65 are sharing housing with nonrelatives (8).

Public Housing Programs

Primarily through the Department of Housing and Urban Development, but also through the Farmers Home Administration of the Department of Agriculture, the federal government has provided construction and operating funds for building and managing housing projects for low-income older persons across the country. Eligibility has been determined principally by age and amount of income, although any age person with physical disabilities is eligible. Rent has been set at no more than 30% of income.

Housing units are generally of three types: no-bedroom (efficiency), one-bedroom, and two-bedrooms. These units are located in high- and low-rise buildings. The projects may be large or small. Sponsors may be nonprofit private groups, public housing authorities, civic organizations, and other public agencies. The objective of these programs has been to provide affordable housing for older persons, with two general needs: fully independent living and limited social support, such as housekeeping help, personal services, recreational activities, and transportation.

An additional kind of housing assistance offered through the federal government is the Section 8 Rental Assistance Program, which provides funds through "Certificates of Eligibility" and "Vouchers." With these documents in hand, obtained from the local housing authority, older persons can locate a suitable housing unit in the community. The housing authority then inspects the unit and negotiates rental arrangements with the owner of the selected unit, including a housing assistance payment contract. Eligibility includes an income that does not exceed 50% of the median income for the community. Older persons' portion of the rent cannot exceed 30% of their income. The housing authority pays the difference from federal funds to the property owner. These programs are believed to be less costly to the federal government than new housing construction programs.

The future of public housing programs is unclear, in view of the federal budget deficits. One proposed federal action is the sale of public housing units to the residents, at reduced prices. Not only would home ownership be encouraged, but the government would be relieved of operating costs. Another proposal is the sale of public housing to private operators.

Supportive Housing Options for Semidependent and Dependent Older Persons

Supportive housing options are for older persons who require more assistance with the routine activities of daily living, whose physical capabilities are diminished, or whose resistance to disease has been reduced. As individuals grow older, they often require easy access to medical services; as a result, they look for supportive housing, which makes such services readily available.

The popular image of supportive housing is a nursing home, the reports about which are often far from favorable. Yet few older persons actually live in nursing homes at any point in time—about 5% of the total population over 65 years of age. The average age of those in nursing homes is presently about 85 years. And the quality of nursing homes and the services they render has greatly improved as a result of state government regulations and the acquisition of large numbers of nursing homes by for-profit national health organizations interested in maintaining operating standards that will enhance the marketability of their nursing homes.

As a matter of fact, studies of aging problems have emphasized at least two important points regarding health care for older persons and their housing needs (9). The first is the importance of appropriate preventive measures to maintain better physical and mental health. The second is the use of all reasonable means to maintain older persons in their own homes for as long as possible.

Examples of prevention measures include the availability of regular medical physical examinations and of wellness programs that involve reasonable amounts of physical exercise, appropriate diet, participation in community life, and avoidance of stress. An example of maintaining older persons in their own homes is illustrated by Florida's Community Care for the Elderly Program, which focuses appropriate community services on particular needs of older persons, maintaining them in their own homes as long as possible.

More and more retirement communities are including "health clinics" or facilities similar to those provided by nursing homes for the residents who find they need these services. The objective of the management in these communities is to strive to improve the condition of the patient so that the patient can return to his or her housing unit.

There are various kinds of supportive housing options: board and care homes; congregate housing, sometimes known as adult congregate living facilities (ACLFs); continuing care retirement communities; and nursing homes (10). Selection of one of these options is based on the needs to be met of preparing food, taking care of maintenance responsibilities at home, having ready access to medical services, and associating with other older persons with similar interests. The mutual involvement of older persons and their adult children in the process of selection and decision will prove beneficial to all those concerned.

Board and Care Homes

Board and care homes provide a familylike atmosphere in which others are living and with whom meals and other activities are shared. The rent includes room, board, utilities, housekeeping and laundry, and concerned staff members who are available to assist with daily living.

Additional fees will provide additional services, such as assistance in bathing and social and recreational activities. Board and care homes are also known as "sheltered housing" or "residential care facilities." Since the quality of service varies, interested older persons should personally assess the situation, talking with some of the residents, and making sure that services as described are written specifically into the contract.

Congregate Housing

As the name implies, congregate housing means association with other older persons in the routine activities of daily living. Although each person has his or her private apartment or room, all residents have the opportunity to eat together in a common dining room. Congregate facilities range in size from about 35 to 300 units. They differ from board and care units in the numbers of residents and the professional or semiprofessional background of staff who are responsible for services and activities.

In some states, including Florida, this type of housing is known as ACLFs. As of 1986, in Florida, there were 47,000 beds in 1,300 facilities licensed by the state. These units may be located in low- or high-rise buildings or in converted homes. They may be part of a retirement community that includes a variety of housing types. Nursing services are not generally available. Very helpful would be units at a level between regular ACLFs and nursing homes for the purpose of meeting the needs of older persons who have special physical problems but do not require the skilled services of a nursing home.

The advantages of congregate housing are the services available in a unit that provides personal privacy, arrangements for health and nutrition programs that support the residents' health and well-being, and companionship and group activities. The result is a personal sense of security, with help available if needed.

Continuing Care Retirement Communities

Continuing care retirement facilities are similar to retirement communities except that they provide skilled nursing services. These communities, first started in the 1920s, were called "life-care communities." However, some 40 in the country ran into serious financial difficulties in the 1970s to the extent that they gave very negative reputations to this type of housing (8). As a consequence, developers adopted a different name, "continuing care retirement communities." One of the problems of the continuing care retirement facilities was the very large up-front nonrefundable entrance fees ranging from $25,000 to $100,000.

Currently, developers tend to offer partial refunds of these fees should the resident move out. Some follow a policy of pay-as-you-go for health care. Overall, monthly charges range from about $650 to $1,200.

The great advantage of the continuing care retirement communities is that older persons who join can be guaranteed housing and services, including health care, for as long as they live. Because concern over illness and the ability to care for themselves is often on the minds of older persons, this type of housing arrangement gives them a real sense of personal security. In view of the variety of policies and fee structures adopted by these housing communities, older persons should examine carefully the conditions and limitations of the contract to which they commit themselves upon becoming residents. They should also inspect the facilities and services offered, to make sure these meet their expectations. Many of these communities are most attractive and the services measure up well. To be checked also is the financial history and condition of the operating organization, since the commitment may be for the rest of the older person's life. Another good point about these communities: It is in the interests of both management and residents for residents to be helped back to reasonable good health in as short a time as possible, and to be able to return from the health clinic (nursing facility) to their housing units. Further, when one member of a married couple needs nursing care, the other can remain in the housing unit, yet be in proximity to the spouse in the nursing facility. Some states have taken legislative action to provide basic regulations governing the operation of these communities.

Nursing Homes

As a type of supportive housing, nursing homes have suffered generally from a public relations problem. This problem has grown out of the conditions found in some nursing homes in the country, as well as the impersonal treatment reported by the residents of various of these homes. Perhaps the most serious charge leveled against nursing homes is that they often deprive residents of their sense of individuality.

However, nursing homes meet a definite need of those older persons who require special extended health care and can no longer live independently. The two levels of care provided are intermediate and skilled. Skilled care is for those who need intensive care but not hospitalization; intermediate care is for those unable to live independently but not needing intensive care. Additional services usually include custodial care and personal care that covers help with meals, bathing, and grooming. Some nursing homes have counseling services, occupational and physical therapy, and recreational activities.

As of 1985, about 1.5 million persons lived in 19,100 nursing homes in the United States; some 75% of these homes re certified to take residents under the Medicare and Medicaid programs. In 1986, these programs contributed about $16.4 billion to the operating costs of these nursing homes—about one-half of their total costs (11). Nursing homes are licensed by state governments and inspected at least once a year; they are usually for-profit organizations.

The cost of a stay in a nursing home ranges from \$12,000 to \$50,000 per year (12). As a result, residents typically exhaust their savings and personal assets within short periods of time, on average within 13 weeks after admission (12), and must apply for Medicaid, a government insurance program for the poor.

When older persons are considering a nursing home, they should explore the answers to such questions as these:

1 Is it really necessary to have nursing home care? Are there other options? What is the recommendation of the individual's physician?

2 What type of care is needed? Is 24-hr supervision necessary, or will a minimum level of care be adequate?

3 How will the nursing home costs be financed? Have the individual's financial resources been properly assessed? To what government assistance program is the individual entitled?

4 Have the older person and his or her family examined a number of nursing homes within a geographical area and learned about ownership, staffing, and facilities available? Have they read the admissions contract and had it reviewed by competent legal authority?

Advance observation can give much helpful information about a nursing home and how it is operated. For example, indifferent attitudes on the part of staff, a minimum of housekeeping standards, disagreeable odors, and marginal maintenance of equipment and facilities all suggest operating limitations of concern. The extent of resident involvement in organizational activity is another indicator of a satisfactory administrative structure.

Well-run nursing homes have varied activities programs, a staff focused on helping residents as individuals, friendly relationships with family members, and physical facilities that create a pleasant living environment. A 1982 report on experiments conducted in nursing homes concluded that residents responded very positively when they were given more responsibilities and encouraged to arrive at their own decisions. The success of these experiments was related to the emphasis placed on the connection between what the residents did and what happened to them and by mindful rather than mindless involvement in their environments (13).

CURRENT HOUSING ISSUES

Housing for older persons is a highly complex subject, because of the many diverse elements involved: the people, their backgrounds, their state of health, financing, rehabilitation, and essential supportive services. In addition, the housing needs and preferences of the older persons change over time, often substantially. Among the current housing issues, at least three are of particular concern: the need for information, the role of housing in maintaining independent living for older adults, and the availability of appropriate and affordable housing for older Americans.

Need for Information

Even though older adults have decided to remain in the family home, information may be needed regarding supportive services, what is available and how they may be obtained when required. Sometimes advice can be very helpful as to courses of action that might be taken to resolve changing circumstances. Often, older adults can consult with a professional counselor who has a wide range of experience with the kinds of housing problems older adults are facing.

When older adults have decided to leave the family home, a number of questions must be answered—Where shall we move? Shall we look for a warmer climate, south or west? What kind of housing do we prefer? Shall we look for a retirement community? Do we prefer a house or an apartment, in a condominium or a cooperative? Will we feel better to have health care services and facilities available? Are community services conveniently located? Will the costs fit our budget? Visiting possible sites and gathering information carefully will enable the persons to make wise choices and decisions.

Sources of information in a community include the area agency on aging, the senior center, the chamber of commerce, and the city hall. When going to a different state, older persons frequently write the State Office on Aging, usually located in the state capitol.

Maintaining an Independent Lifestyle

Most older persons maintain an independent lifestyle in retirement, living in their family homes or moving to smaller houses or apartments. A relatively small percentage move south or west to a warmer climate. Some older persons find themselves living alone, and some lose their health and become physically frail.

In the last instance the first reaction of family members or friends is often that these frail or unwell older persons should move to a nursing home. This reaction should be replaced by asking and answering the question "What kind of housing would best meet the needs of this particular individual?" As noted earlier, nursing homes are designed for dependent older persons. The alternatives should be considered and the selection made in favor of the one that best enables the older person to maintain maximum independence in lifestyle. Often his or her own home is the one selected, when adequate supportive services can be provided there. This selection is usually a less expensive choice.

Affordable Housing

Housing is expensive. In 1987, the national median sales price for a new home was $92,000 (14). For older persons who are selling their homes and moving to another area, this situation means that they can hope to sell their old home at an inflated price, compared with the original purchase price, which might cover the inflated price of a new home or apartment, depending on what sections of the country are involved.

At the lower end of the economic ladder, more than 71% of low-income renters, regardless of age, were paying more than 35% of their income for rent in 1987. Some 11.6 million persons were living in substandard housing, and 16.5% lived in run-down neighborhoods (15). Some 3.3 million older persons were living below the poverty level in 1984 (defined as $6,282 for an older couple) (2). This information suggests that older persons of low and low to moderate income often live in unsatisfactory housing and many find that housing constitutes for them a major problem.

A number of states use general revenue funds for various housing programs and services for older persons. Some have developed special trust funds for use in housing programs. Such funds are often intended to encourage new construction by private developers. Federal funds and federal programs are still relied on, although these sources of support are largely gone.

The affordability of housing also involves its adaptability to meet the changing needs of older persons as they age. These needs include easy accessibility to rooms and to room storage spaces and safety features such as grab bars in the bathroom, nonskid floor materials, and adequate illumination. The Department of Housing and Urban Development has published a manual that developers of housing, managers, and consumers will find useful (15).

IMPLICATIONS FOR COUNSELORS

The topic of housing has several implications for counselors assisting older persons. Perhaps most important is knowledge of the various alternatives and the impact that the housing environment has on the well-being of older persons, including their sense of independence. Understanding the physical condition of counselees and any limitations placed thereby on their abilities and capacities is vital.

Knowledge of what kinds of housing accommodations and what support services are available in the community where the older person lives is also essential. Particularly relevant is the ability to assist with financial planning, in terms of sources of funds and total expenses involved. The elements that contribute to a quality housing environment should also be studied and their relative importance evaluated.

GROUP ACTIVITIES

Divide the group into groups of four to six participants and assign a leader to each group. The group leader should open up the discussion by asking if individual members are familiar with problems faced by older persons in connection with their housing, and how these problems might be approached. Additional approaches might be suggested during this discussion.

1 Individual members should be asked to describe what kinds of retirement housing arrangements they would want to make for themselves, at some future date.

2 The group leader would encourage a general group discussion on physical disabilities faced by some older persons and how these disabilities could affect the kinds of housing in which older persons might live.

3 The group leader might ask the group to plan a retirement housing project which would best meet the needs of older persons. What supportive services should be provided? What facilities might be included that would enable older persons experiencing some disabilities to remain in their units for extended periods?

An experienced developer and an architect who has designed retirement housing might be invited to serve as consultants for the group activities.

REFERENCES

1 U. S. Senate Special Committee on Aging. (1985–1986). *Aging America, trends and projections.* Washington, DC: U. S. Department of Health and Human Services.

2 U. S. Senate Special Committee on Aging. (1987–1988). *Aging America, trends and projections.* Washington, DC: U. S. Department of Health and Human Services.

3 American Association of Retired Persons. (1986). *Understanding senior housing.* Washington, DC: Author.

4 Carp, F. M. (1966). *A future for the aged: Victoria Plaza and its residents.* Austin, TX: University of Texas Press.

5 Butler, R. M., & Lewis, M. I. (1982). *Aging and mental health: Positive psychosocial and biomedical approaches.* St. Louis: C. V. Mosby.

6 Carp, F. M. (1976). Housing and Living Environments of Older People. In R. G. Binstock & E. Shanas (Eds.), *Handbook of aging and the social sciences.* New York: Van Nostrand Reinhold.

7 Hubbard, L. (Ed.). (1984). *Housing options for older Americans.* Washington, DC: American Association of Retired Persons.

8 Steinberg, N. (1987, May/June). No place like home. *Mature Outlook, 4*(3), 84–89.

9 Florida Committee on Aging. (1986). *Pathways to the future.* Tallahassee, FL: Department of Health and Rehabilitative Services.

10 American Association of Retired Persons. (1985). *Your home, your choice.* Washington, DC: Author.

11 Strahan, G. (1987). *Nursing home characteristics, preliminary data from 1985 national nursing home survey. Advance data.* Washington, DC: U. S. Department of Health and Human Services, Public Health Services.

12 U. S. Senate Special Committee on Aging. (1987). *Developments in aging: 1986. Vol. 1.* Washington, DC: U. S. Government Printing Office.

13 Beck, P. (1982). Two successful interventions in nursing homes: The therapeutic effects of cognitive activity. *The Gerontologist, 22*(4), 378–383.

14 State of Florida. (1987, November 20). *Final draft report, Affordable housing study commission.* Tallahassee, FL: Department of Community Affairs.

15 Bostrom, J. A., Mace, R. L., & Long, M. (1987). *Adaptable housing.* Washington, DC: U. S. Department of Housing and Urban Development.

Chapter Nine

Financing a New Lifestyle

In previous chapters we have examined the variety of roles and activities that are possible for persons in their retirement years. This chapter explores basic information to help retirees finance the lifestyle they choose. In fact, finances and health rank as the most critical factors in determining retirement satisfaction (1). In the words of one retiree, "Retirement has many attractions, . . . but if one cannot afford them in retirement what good is retirement? Having the time to do things is little satisfaction if one cannot afford to pursue them" (2, p. 90).

Across all income ranges, people have to make some financial adjustments to retirement (1). For most persons, retirement is accompanied by a one-half to two-thirds drop in income. That's one-half to two-thirds less than most people couldn't quite live on before! The shift occurs from one day to the next, from the day in which one is working to the next day when one is retired. This dramatic shift captures people's attention and imagination. At least one other important financial implication of the retirement years is given secondary (if any) attention: Expenses also tend to decrease in later life, for some persons significantly.

It is fairly self-evident and has been empirically established that planning in advance for financial needs in later life is not only desirable but essential (1–4). Those who want to maximize their choice of lifestyle are most successful when retirement planning begins in young adulthood or midlife. However, it is never too late to begin evaluating and planning one's financial needs and resources. The purpose of this chapter is to explore the various components of financial planning and examine options available to retirees.

The first section provides an overview of the economic status of older Americans. The importance of financial planning is stressed in the subsequent sections, which include discussions of six major planning steps or strategies for retirement financial planning (3). These steps include estimating expenses, determining sources and amount of income, comparing income with expenses, establishing funds to counteract inflation, evaluating current assets, and conducting financial planning to improve one's financial condition. A discussion of estate planning and implications for counselors are included at the end of the chapter.

ECONOMIC STATUS OF OLDER AMERICANS

The high cost of living and inflation top the list of the most serious problems facing older persons (1). In addition, lack of money, lack of retirement income, general financial problems, and not having enough money to live on are concerns of persons over the age of 65. Increasing numbers of older persons are feeling threats to their incomes and financial security.

Those having the lowest incomes (under $5,000 per year) and minorities are most in agreement that the financial well-being of older Americans has declined in the last two decades. Only 41% of White Americans agree that this is so. Some 17% of all older Americans experience lack of money as a very serious problem. This includes 13% of White older Americans, 42% of older Blacks, and 52% of older Hispanics. A majority of older White persons (52%) are "getting by with a little extra or buying pretty much anything they want with their present incomes [whereas] large majorities of blacks (80%) and Hispanics (71%) are just scraping by or are in real financial difficulty" (1, p. 70).

Median income levels decline consistently with age. The highest median income in 1981 was $22,400 for persons aged 18–64. This was in contrast to a low of $6,000 among persons over age 80 (1). Studies of retirement cash flow show sharp drops as a function of age, with persons over 80 receiving the lowest incomes (5). Many older persons receive lower incomes based on pensions paid during times when salaries were much lower—in the 1950s, 1960s, and 1970s (2). For others, especially women and minorities, access to high-paying jobs was restricted during most of the 1900s.

Even with advances in the status of women in the labor market, the future financial status of women is uncertain. Some researchers argue that older men will continue to be better off than older women, particularly those who live alone. Quinlan (6) noted that 38% of men living alone are poor or nearly poor now and projected that this rate will decline to 6% by the year 2020. In contrast, the proportion of older women who are poor or nearly poor will drop only from 45% to 38% in the next 30 years.

A study of 1,500 retirees by the Teacher Insurance and Annuity Association, College Retirement Equities Fund (TIAA–CREF) (2) revealed that most retirees do not perceive their incomes as small in the perspective of their life earnings. Slightly more than one-fourth of the TIAA–CREF retirees had incomes under $15,000 per year, one-fourth had incomes between $15,000 and $20,000, one-fourth had incomes between $25,000 and $40,000, and just under one-fourth had incomes over $40,000. Most felt they were living well, with 30% reporting their financial situation to be better than before retirement, half about the same, and 15% reporting they were worse off after retirement. It should be noted that the TIAA–CREF retirees, on the whole, have higher incomes that many older persons, particularly those who depend on Social Security and Supplemental Security Income.

One conclusion of the TIAA–CREF study was that people eventually adjust to their income level, regardless of what it is, so long as it does not drop drastically. The purpose of financial planning, of course, is to ensure that one's income during retirement is adequate, in the long term, to meet one's needs. The remainder of this chapter is devoted to a consideration of financial planning for the later years.

FINANCIAL PLANNING FOR RETIREMENT

Financial planning is a process that allows individuals to take better control of their financial assets and manage their money more effectively (7). The first step in preparing for a secure retirement income is to set financial goals to achieve certain objectives (7, 8). These goals could include having more dollars to spend, finding ways to expand dollars and sources of income (e.g., growth of assets), and protecting assets and lifestyle (9). A number of steps may be required to determine appropriate goals, and a variety of persons–financial planners, insurance agents, accountants, stock brokers, bankers, and counselors— may be helpful in the planning process.

Weaver and Buchanan (4) recommended that retirees concentrate on their dreams and desires when setting financial goals. Factors to consider are where the person wants to live, what kind of people the person wants to be with, how close the person wants to be to other members of his or her family (children, parents, siblings, and relatives), what kind of activities the person wants to pursue, whether the person wants to work full or part time, how and where the person wants to develop skills and knowledge, and what the person would like to accomplish during his or her life. These and other important issues in planning retirement lifestyle are discussed throughout this book. This chapter focuses on financing the lifestyle that is chosen.

Six important steps in financial planning are discussed below. It is helpful to the individual going through these steps to use a financial planning worksheet that allows listing of income and expenses and projection of changes based on changes in either of these categories (3). Examples of such worksheets may be found in publications by the American Association for Retired Persons (9–11) and are available through financial institutions such as banks and savings and loan associations.

DETERMINING EXPENSES

Retirement planning includes a concurrent determination of expenses and income. When expenses exceed income, then additional sources of income must be identified or expenses reduced. When income exceeds expenses, additional lifestyle options may be explored.

As mentioned earlier, the drop in income most retirees experience is accompanied by a decrease in expenses. However, many expenses are under the control of retirees. For example, expenses will vary depending on where and how persons choose to live. Some retirement communities or condominiums with recreational programs and services can be very expensive, whereas other living arrangements, including some mobile home communities in the Sunbelt regions, may cost an amount equal to Social Security income. Many retired persons have paid-up mortgages by the time they retire, educational expenses for children have been completed, expenses for travel to and from work and work lunches are decreased or eliminated, and expenses for purchases of work clothing decrease. Income tax liability decreases. In general, work-related expenses will decrease and some adjustment in spending habits will be required.

Planning for retirement expenses involves a determination of current expenses as well as projected expenses after retirement. The Educational Technology Corporation (3) has recommended using different projections based on the length of time remaining until retirement. If retiring within 2 years or so, estimated costs may be realistic. The further away from retirement one is when planning, the less useful will be detailed budgets because they are more subject to change.

Inflation (discussed in Step 4, below) will, of course, affect projections and is impossible to predict. Therefore, when planning for postretirement expenses, some attention to the effects of inflation is necessary. Expenses to consider include costs for basic living, such as housing, food, clothing, transportation, taxes, and medical payments. Additional costs may be for insurance, debts, leisure activities, education, and gifts. Once expenses have been determined and sources of income identified, the next step is to develop a budget.

Table 1   Average Annual Expenditures of Urban Consumer Units by Type of Expenditure and Age of Household: 1984

| | Percentage distribution | | |
Type of expenditure	Under 65	65–74	75 +
Shelter/furnishings	22.9	20.2	23.8
Utilities	7.3	10.4	11.7
Food	15.3	17.8	17.1
Clothing	5.7	4.5	3.1
Health care	3.3	8.4	13.3
Transportation	20.5	19.2	13.0
Pension and life insurance	10.0	4.9	2.0
Entertainment	5.0	3.8	2.6
Cash contributions	7.0	6.0	5.6
Other	3.1	4.8	7.8

Note.   Adapted from U.S. Bureau of Labor Statistics. (1986). *Consumer expenditure survey: Interview survey, 1984* (Bulletin No. 2267). Washington, DC: U.S. Department of Labor.

Developing a Budget

In developing a budget, it might be helpful to know where most retirees spend their monies. Table 1 provides an indication of sources of expenditures for older adults compared with younger adults. It is noteworthy that expenditures by older adults tend to go down except in the categories of housing, food, and health care. Health care expenditures tend to increase.

Many or even most retirees live on a fixed income. Developing a budget can be an effective means for making maximum use of available funds. Part of establishing a budget involves determining income and expenses to meet basic living needs. Another part is determining goals for a desired lifestyle, then examining how one's budget can be used to finance that lifestyle. Budgets need to be examined per month as well as per year.

Any budget begins with fixed expenses to meet basic living needs, though even these can be somewhat flexible. For example, the costs of home ownership as opposed to living in an apartment or condominium can be assessed. Cooking fresh foods as opposed to cooking processed foods or eating out can make significant differences in the food budget.

Goals for leisure, for example, need to include both long- and short-range planning. Some persons choose to spend a little money each week on a favorite activity, such as eating out, going to a movie, or playing bingo. Others choose to stay home most of the time, then spend several hundred or thousand dollars on a major trip. Leisure planning, including trips to visit relatives and educational programs, is an important component for determining a budget.

Sometimes one's goals, desires, and plans exceed the scope of one's budget. Sometimes emergencies arise, such as unexpected illnesses, which deplete financial reserves. For whatever other reasons, it is desirable for most retirees to examine potential sources of income (Step 2) and ways to improve their financial situation (Step 6).

IDENTIFYING INCOME

The second step in planning finances during retirement is to identify sources of income. "Income helps determine the flexibility a retiree has to choose a retirement lifestyle; the higher the income, the greater the options" (2, p. 92). The American Association of Retired Persons (AARP) (11) has identified eight possible sources of income for retirees: Social Security, private pensions, do-it-yourself pensions, annuities, savings, stocks and bonds, real estate, and employment earnings. Yet another possible source is income provided through or by family members. These are discussed below.

The income sources discussed here represent the major sources of income to retirees. Other sources may be considered for some persons in some instances. Perlmutter (12) offered a detailed list of potential sources of income and suggestions for enhancing retirement income. Among the possible sources of income he considered are government annuities, veteran's pensions, private pensions, Social Security, deferred profit sharing, private annuities, life insurance cash value, investment dividends, savings account interest, interest from bonds, capital gains, rents, payments from mortgages the person holds, part-time jobs, earnings from self-employment, Individual Retirement Accounts (IRAs), Keoghs, all-savers, and bequests, windfalls, and so forth.

Social Security and Supplemental Security Income

Social Security benefits, although available to most persons who have worked, cover only minimal expenses for most older persons. These benefits are not automatic; rather, the retiree must apply for them. The process can be confusing, so it is recommended that persons approaching retirement collect and study all available pamphlets and written materials to assist them in determining their eligibility for benefits (4, 13). Some sources of information are listed in the references at the end of this chapter.

The Social Security system was designed as a basic insurance policy to replace family earnings lost because of retirement, death, or disability of primary wage earners. Eligibility requires the worker to have been employed a certain number of quarters (3-month periods) of the year, with the number of quarters varying according to the age and disability status of the individual upon application. Disability benefits may be provided for persons under age 65 if they are permanently and totally disabled, having a disability that will last more than one year. Benefits do not begin until 6 months after the onset of the disability, and there are no retroactive benefits for the first 6 months. When disabled persons reach retirement age, their benefits are automatically converted to retirement benefits with no loss in income.

Survivor's benefits are available to widows and widowers, unmarried children, dependent parents, and divorced spouses. A lump-sum death benefit usually is paid to survivors for the purpose of paying for funeral and burial expenses. The laws regarding payment of benefits to older women are complex. Sometimes women can choose whether to collect benefits based on their own work or that of their husband; they would be wise to explore the options and choose the higher possible income.

Establishing eligibility for Social Security is necessary for receiving Medicare services, the federal program of health care for older persons. Medicare includes Part A, hospital insurance, and Part B, physician and surgeon charges both in and out of the hospital. If older persons have sufficient retirement credits for work under Social Security, they are eligible for Part A whether or not they choose to retire. People who are not eligible must pay a monthly premium for Part A and Part B coverage. Since Medicare rules may change, there is a waiting period for eligibility while papers are processed, and some expenses may not be retroactive to the age of 65. Persons under age 65 and nearing retirement are encouraged to apply for benefits at least 3 months prior to retirement.

Those older persons who can establish financial need, including persons over 65 whose Social Security earnings are low, as well as those who are under 65 but have blindness or another disability, may be eligible for Supplemental Security Income (SSI). The basic purpose of SSI is to assure that everyone in the United States has a certain minimum household income. Persons who receive SSI also are eligible for Medicaid, which pays for some medical expenses that Medicare does not cover. Medigap insurances also pay for expenses not covered by Medicare. These coverages are available through private insurance companies.

The Social Security regulations include a ceiling on earnings. If a person works and earns more than a certain amount each year, his or her Social Security benefits will be reduced or terminated. This does not apply to older persons age 70 or above or to some income from other sources, such as pensions and savings. Such additional income will affect SSI payments, however, because it is considered in determining need for this benefit program. It is important for retirees to learn the current laws in relation to earnings, taxes on Social Security and other income, eligibility for SSI and other benefits, and other aspects of the Social Security laws in order to take full advantage of available benefits. The laws do change, sometimes working to the retiree's advantage and other times to his or her detriment.

Private (Employer-Sponsored) Pensions

Private pensions are available to increasing numbers of workers. Most large companies now have pension plans and provide employees with annual pension statements. In fact, these annual statements are required by law. Personnel departments can assist older workers in determining their benefits and entitlements, including consideration for changing benefits based on remaining years left to work.

Benefits statements should be carefully considered in reference to the following (3): the age it is assumed one will retire, the payment option or options it is assumed one will choose, and whether the plan assumes one will opt for a survivor's benefit. The assumptions used to prepare plans are based on the situation common to most persons. So, if the retiree's situation differs from most other persons, these assumptions may need to be changed.

Many retirees assume that their pension and Social Security benefits will be adequate for living in their retirement years. This assumption is not always true. Workers need to fully understand their pension plans, especially the provisions for becoming "vested." It is sad but true that many expected pensions have not materialized for retirees because of factors such as inadequate funding, failure of businesses or employers, merger with another company, and loss of job before full vesting has occurred. Some pension plans have cost-of-living raises as a built-in component, whereas others provide a fixed income regardless of inflation. Pension plans available to many older persons include Veterans Benefits, Civil Service Retirement, and Railroad Retirement.

Do-It-Yourself Pensions

Do-it-yourself pensions are a fairly recent phenomenon, receiving impetus from the Economic Recovery Act of 1981. Before that time, IRAs were available only to workers not covered by pension plans at their place of employment (11). Now any worker who is earning an income can establish an IRA, and the maximum amounts that one can invest have increased. Following the Tax Reform Act of 1986, only lower income workers and those not covered by company pension plans can make tax-deductible contributions to an IRA (8). All contributions receive tax-deferred interest until the money is withdrawn. The basic premise is that persons will not withdraw monies until retirement, when they are in lower tax brackets, so withdrawal from IRA accounts is not permitted until age 59½.

Persons over the age of 60 or 65 who are still working may benefit from starting an IRA. After the age of 59½, part or all of an IRA can be withdrawn without penalty. The account balance will continue to grow even if withdrawals are made, based on the remaining funds. Upon retirement, IRAs can be withdrawn in a lump sum, placed in an annuity, or withdrawn in installments. There are tax consequences to each option.

Keogh plans are recommended for persons who are self-employed (8). In contrast to IRAs, Keogh contributions may be made as long as an income is earned from self-employment, even after age 70. The rules for withdrawal from Keogh plans and IRAs are the same.

It is possible to establish retirement accounts for a spouse as well as oneself. Persons interested in do-it-yourself pensions can obtain assistance from banks, savings and loan associations, insurance companies, mutual funds, and stock brokerage firms.

Annuities

Annuities are a type of savings plan sometimes described as reverse life insurance. An annuity plan is purchased which allows one to make cash payments to a financial institution, which in turn provides monthly payments to the retiree for as long as he or she lives. The amount of payment per $1,000 invested is less for women than for men because of the longer life span of women. Some annuities pay a specified amount per month and others (variable annuities) pay a varying amount to help retirees keep pace with inflation. There are many types of annuities, and the benefits provided vary among the many companies providing them.

Annuities provide a guaranteed income for life. Persons reaching retirement age may purchase an immediate annuity and begin receiving payments at once, usually using funds from the IRA or Keogh plan to purchase the annuity. Payment options for annuities vary and should be carefully considered. A decision must be made whether a dependent spouse may continue to receive benefits after the death of an annuitant. Straight-life annuities provide payments to an annuitant until his or her death and no benefits to survivors. Joint and survivor annuities pay income to one or more survivors of an annuitant.

The AARP has summarized several advantages of annuities for retirees (14): It frees the retiree or worker of the task of money management; the individual can never outlive his or her capital; it makes saving for older age easier while making it hard to use savings prior to older age; and annuities draw interest during a person's working years, but allow for withdrawal during retirement when the person is in a lower tax bracket.

Savings

Savings are a source of income for many retirees. Stoller and Stoller (15) suggested that older persons have a propensity to save for a number of reasons. Chief among these are concerns for adequacy of income and financial security. Concerns about health and medical expenses are another important reason to save.

There are a number of ways to save money, and also various institutions through which to save. Savings are not restricted to personal savings accounts.

Money may be saved through purchases of certificates of deposit and savings bonds, for example, and also through investments in savings plans. Since the benefits and restrictions to savings plans vary considerably, it is important to explore various options before making a firm financial commitment.

Banks, savings and loan associations, and credit unions may offer a bewildering assortment of options for savings, each with different names, conditions, and investment yields. Savings are protected when banks are insured by the Federal Deposit Insurance Corporation and when savings and loan associations are insured by the Federal Savings and Loan Insurance Corporation. Stocks and bonds, discussed below, are major options for saving money.

Stocks and Bonds

Stocks and bonds are another potential source of income for retirees. It is wise to consult an investment broker prior to purchase of stocks, bonds, or mutual funds. Bonds are the least risky purchase because they include a set amount of repayment according to a predetermined schedule. The return from stocks and mutual funds, including money market mutual funds, is not always predictable. Investors have both gained money and lost money through such investments.

The safest of all securities are those available through the U. S. government. Interest paid on any government security is free from state and local taxes (9). The most common securities are Treasury Bills, Treasury Notes, and EE and HH U. S. Savings Bonds. Treasury Bills may be purchased for 3 or 6 months or 1 year, while EE and HH bonds mature in 10 years. Federal taxes on yields are deferred until the bonds mature or are redeemed.

A variety of money market funds that are not common stocks are also available. These are sold through banks, savings and loan associations, and investment firms. Because of the tremendous variety of options for purchase and the variability in yields, it is helpful to discuss intended purchases with a financial adviser. Not all money market funds are insured, and some represent a financial risk in that the amount of funds taken out may end up being less than that invested, or not as great a yield as was desired or promised.

Real Estate and Mortgage Investments

Real estate has long been considered a sound financial investment. Home ownership is one component of this investment process. Retirees may elect to sell their homes to help finance another lifestyle. Investment in other real estate, such as homes, apartments, shopping centers, or undeveloped land, can result in substantial earnings. However, the investment of time and effort in property management must be balanced against projected gains. Many persons build their retirement income on property investments, usually beginning in midlife.

Another option is to invest in government-sponsored mortgage investments, popularly known as Ginnie Maes and Freddie Macs. Ginnie Maes, issued by the Government National Mortgage Association, are securities issued by organizations that comply with certain government regulations. Payments are guaranteed by the U. S. government. These offer high yields with excellent risk protection (9). Freddie Mac is a government corporation that combines conventional home mortgages into pools. Both of these investments are offered in units of $100,000 only. However, some specialized mutual funds invest in Ginnie Maes. Again, the services of a financial consultant will be useful to anyone planning to invest in real estate mortgages.

Employment

Employment to gain additional income is discussed in detail in Chapter 7. Retirees may elect full- or part-time employment. They may choose to work for others or be self-employed. Earnings restrictions of Social Security need to be considered in choosing employment, as well as other aspects of lifestyle discussed throughout this book.

Family Members

Income provided through family members is a source of funds for a minority of older persons. Conversely, many older persons receive financial gifts from relatives, yet this income is not essential to meet basic living needs. Where such assistance is available, and can be consistently expected, it should be included in retirement planning.

Another consideration in regard to relatives is other-than-cash contributions. Assistance in home care, meals preparation, transportation, or other services should be included in preparation of retirement budgets. The assistance of family members may be especially important in times of emergency, such as an unexpected illness.

COMPARING INCOME WITH EXPENSES

The third major step in retirement planning, after developing a statement of expenses and considering potential sources of income, is a comparison of income with expenses. The outcome of this comparison will determine if one's projected income will be adequate to cover anticipated expenses after retirement. If income exceeds anticipated expenses, then there will be a cushion against unexpected expenses.

If currently determined retirement income is insufficient to cover projected expenses, then preretirement planning must include consideration of additional ways to produce income. When the effects of inflation, considered below, are included, the shortfall may be even greater than anticipated. On the other hand, current assets may help to offset any shortfall. Thus, a consideration of liquidation of assets, also discussed below, becomes an important part of retirement financial planning.

ESTABLISHING FUNDS TO COUNTERACT INFLATION

The rate of inflation in the United States has risen to unprecedented levels in recent decades. As measured by the consumer price index (CPI), it is unlikely that the inflation rate will drop below 6% per year for the rest of the century, a figure that is considered conservative by many persons (5). When older persons state that their standard of living has continued to drop during retirement, the effects of inflation make this statement correct. Persons with low and fixed incomes are particularly affected by inflation (2).

Pay increases for workers are tied, to some extent, to increases in the CPI. Increases for retirees, on the other hand, are tied to pay in the years preceding retirement. Pension calculations, in other words, keep up with the inflation that occurs before a person retires (3). Inflation after retirement is much more of a concern.

Many pension plans are fixed, so that the amount a person receives does not change at all after retirement regardless of inflation or increases in the CPI. When older persons complain of *fixed incomes,* it means that their income remains the same while the cost of essential goods increases. It is often an employer's discretion whether to raise a pension payment or not. Such increases are unpredictable.

It is helpful to persons planning for retirement to develop a "personal" inflation rate (3). How one spends one's money helps to determine the personal inflation rate, and many retirees thus have personal rates below the national average. Persons nearing retirement should consider ways to "freeze" or otherwise control assets prone to inflation, such as through home ownership rather than renting, using public transportation rather than purchasing a new automobile, and so forth. Consideration of one's projected life span is a part of this planning. It is a good idea to plan to outlive your money—to live longer than you might expect in order to have sufficient funds for the remainder of one's life.

Two types of funds may be considered to assist retirees in offsetting the effects of inflation. These are indexing funds and whole pension funds (3). Indexing funds are used to supplement fixed pensions by an amount equal to the effects of inflation. Whole pension funds provide a personal pension with a built-in inflation index. Both types of funds are available through a variety of financial institutions and should be personalized to the needs of the retiree.

EVALUATING CURRENT ASSETS

As a general rule, most assets increase in value in proportion to the inflation rate, with the exception of real estate, which has increased more rapidly (3). It is reasonable to assume that a person's assets will increase over time through proper management. An important component of retirement planning is to consider the projected value of assets and how those could be used during the retirement years. If projected asset values are sufficient to meet projected retirement expenses, then that is important to know.

On the other hand, most people engaging in retirement financial planning determine that they need to accumulate more assets to meet projected expenses or provide a buffer against inflation or unanticipated emergencies. Possibilities for generating assets can be discussed with financial planners. Some options to consider are (3) determining if present rates of saving or investing can be increased, reconsidering assumptions about inflation and after-tax earnings, considering paid work during retirement to overcome projected shortfalls, considering delaying retirement until the needed additional assets have been acquired, taking steps to increase the rate of return on savings and other investments, and considering ways to reduce expenses while maintaining a satisfying lifestyle during retirement.

FINANCIAL PLANNING TO IMPROVE ONE'S FINANCIAL CONDITION

Earlier in this chapter nine sources of potential income for retirees were identified. Each of these sources could be used to improve one's financial situation; however, any of them work best when planning occurs earlier in life. Pension and savings plans, for example, require a number of years to reach maturity. Constructive use of credit may aid retirees in making investments. For example, home mortgages can yield cash for real estate or other investment purposes, as can some life insurance policies.

The Educational Technology Corporation (3) stressed the fact that attitude can have an important impact on financial planning. Retirees need to really believe that they can improve their finances in order to implement a plan to do so. Retirees are encouraged to accept responsibility for planning and achieving their own financial security, and to understand that investing is an art. Experts will differ in their opinions, and ultimately the decisions to be made should be made by an informed consumer who has explored a variety of available options. Taking the time to study these options, and to increase the number of choices, will pay off in the long run.

Important issues to consider in planning improvements in one's financial status are discussed in numerous sources (2, 5, 9, 13). These include the need to start or continue to save money, consider current and future tax brackets and after-tax earnings, learn about government provisions for tax benefits to older persons, and learn which assets—Social Security, pensions, bond incomes— might be nontaxable under certain conditions. Retirees can benefit from research into medical insurance policies in preparation for possible increased medical costs.

Investment possibilities should be explored and considered as potential means for increasing incomes after retirement. Those who want to invest would be wise to (a) go slowly and (b) get professional advice prior to investing. Such advice could come from an accountant, banker, or life insurance salesperson. Older persons are frequent victims of crime, with a major area of crime being fraud. Toward the end of the life span, with limited opportunities for employment and lack of access to opportunities to gain additional income, some older persons find themselves ready prey for dishonest schemes. When a lifetime of living and working has not yielded greater wealth, get-rich-quick schemes may have increased appeal. Susceptible individuals may be those who regret not having a greater estate to leave behind to their heirs. It is critical that the credentials of financial planners and institutions be validated prior to any investment being made.

ORGANIZING AN ESTATE PLAN

Persons' estates are defined as the sum of all that they own, plus all that is owed to them, minus all that they owe to others. It also is called one's "net worth" (14). An estate becomes a legal entity at the time of its owner's death. In the absence of binding instructions, which are provided in a will, the estate is subject to distribution according to the laws of the state in which the person resided. Clearly, those who want to have their estate and assets distributed in a set manner *must* have a will (16). In addition, the will can help to eliminate arguments among surviving members of the family.

Planning their estate requires retirees to look ahead and imagine what will happen to all that they own after they die. Sometimes it is helpful to fantasize what is happening the day after one's funeral, and imagine how and where each of one's assets is to be distributed. State and federal taxes, court disputes, and disrupted family relationships can occur when there is not a will. One's intentions are meaningless in the absence of legal documentation. A difficulty here, of course, is that many persons consider thinking about death, especially their own, to be at least distasteful and at most morbid. Therefore, they tend to avoid consideration of planning their estate and writing a will.

Estate planning can be approached from at least two perspectives. One approach is to arrange one's assets so that they may be distributed with ease and limited additional costs. The other is to specify instructions for such distribution, that is, to write a will (14). In either case, retirees will need to define their estate, determine how they would like it distributed, and take steps to ensure that their wishes are legally mandated.

The process of defining an estate requires that one's net worth be examined as it exists currently and as it is projected to exist in the future. Major assets need to be specified, such as home equity, personal property, life insurance, annuities, savings, pensions, and other investments. These assets can be listed in a column on the left side of a piece of blank paper. Using three or more additional columns, retirees can fill in the amount of each asset currently and for projected years in the future. On another page, a budget developed according to guidelines discussed earlier can be used to determine projected liabilities each year. The final figures, assets per year minus liabilities per year, will give an indication of a person's net worth from year to year.

A second part of this process requires defining one's personal property. Again, a list can be made. Beside each item the retiree can indicate who he or she would like to receive that item when the estate is divided. Some retirees choose to list only certain major, sentimental items, then specify that remaining items are to be sold and the proceeds distributed among one's heirs. Another technique is to specify that all of the estate must be liquidated. Relatives wanting to bid on certain items will have first choice prior to public sales.

It is imperative in estate planning to gain professional advice, because laws vary from state to state. Some states recognize living wills, for example, whereas others do not. Handwritten wills are legal in some states, and oral wills are allowed under certain emergency conditions in others. Accountants, bankers, life insurance agents, and lawyers are the primary professionals to consult. Some communities have senior centers and other programs that offer low-cost legal services to retired persons. Legal services will be less costly when retired persons have accomplished the steps suggested above of defining their estate and how they would like it to be distributed.

A comprehensive record-keeping system for estate planning has been developed by the AARP. The publication "Your Vital Papers Logbook" (10) is an excellent resource for examining one's financial situation and planning an estate. Attorneys and life insurance agents may have additional papers for use in such planning. Again, this is an area where some type of professional help will be useful, including the services available through counselors.

IMPLICATIONS FOR COUNSELORS

Counselors working with retirees or persons planning their retirement must include discussion of financial considerations in their work. It is important to remember that some of the issues will be sensitive and clients (or their family members) may resist such discussions. For example, many persons will avoid estate planning in order to avoid thinking about death and dying. Others will avoid estate planning to avoid family arguments. Sometimes a couple will disagree about their estate, and the ensuing stalemate leads to a lack of planning for the family. Counselors need to be prepared to deal with these sensitive issues, and must be willing to explore in depth feelings about death, dying, and survivorship.

As is true for other aspects of retirement planning, counselors must be prepared to function as information and referral agents, linking retirees and preretirees with resources to help them in financial planning. Counselors should be aware of such resources in their community, including insurance agencies, banks and other financial institutions, and legal aid programs. Counselors should be prepared to discuss financial information with their clients, but should not hesitate to suggest referral for additional information.

Should the client be interested specifically in the services of a financial planner, the counselor should suggest that selections be preceded by obtaining detailed information about the planner. This information should include the planner's credentials for practicing financial planning, registration with a state agency or the federal Securities and Exchange Commission, the companies represented by the planner, methods for helping with current or later financial developments, the amount of time available to individual clients, and the fees.

GROUP ACTIVITIES

    I Using the categories listed in Table 1, develop a budget that reflects your current expenses. Compare this with your current income. How might both your income and expenses change during retirement?

   II Review the steps involved in establishing a budget and planning an estate. Take two sheets of paper and mark three columns on each one. In the first column, list the factors important for planning budgets and estates, respectively. In the second column, list your current budgetary needs and assets and liabilities. In the third column, list your projected budgetary needs and estate at age 70 or whatever age you will be retired. Think about and discuss the following questions:

    1 What is the difference between the second and third columns?

    2 How can you use this information to plan effectively for your life in retirement?

    3 How can you use what you have learned in counseling with persons regarding retirement?

REFERENCES

  1 Harris, L., & Associates. (1981). *Aging in the eighties: America in transition.* Washington, DC: National Council on the Aging.

  2 Miletti, M. A. (1984). *Voices of experience: 1500 retired people talk about retire-*

ment. New York: Teachers Insurance and Annuity Association, College Retirement Equities Fund.

3   Educational Technology Corporation. (1981). *Financial planning for retirement.* Silver Spring, MD: Author.

4   Weaver, P., & Buchanan, A. (1984). *What to do with what you've got: The practical guide to money management in retirement.* Glenview, IL: Scott, Foresman.

5   Soldofsky, R. M. (1980). Financial counseling: General economic background and information for helping elderly clients. In C. J. Pulvino & N. Colangelo (Eds.), *Counseling for the growing years: 65 and over* (pp. 131–162). Minneapolis, MN: Educational Media Corporation.

6   Quinlan, A. (1989). Women living alone. *New Choices, 29*(1), 13.

7   IDS Financial Corporation. (1987). *Financial planning: How is works for you.* New York: IDS Life Insurance Company.

8   American Council of Life Insurance. (1987). *Health care and finances: A guide for adult children and their parents.* Washington, DC: Author.

9   American Association of Retired Persons. (1985). *Take charge of your money: Managing your financial resources in retirement.* Washington, DC: Author.

10   American Association of Retired Persons. (1985). *Your vital papers logbook.* Washington, DC: Author.

11   Action for Independent Maturity. (1983). *AIMs guide to financial security.* Washington, DC: American Association of Retired Persons.

12   Perlmutter, E. K. (1983). *Retired, refired.* Washington, DC: Graduate School Press.

13   American Association of Retired Persons. (1977). *Your retirement legal guide.* Washington, DC: Author.

14   American Association of Retired Persons. (1985). *The essential guide to wills, estates, trusts, and death taxes.* Washington, DC: Author.

15   Stoller, E. P., & Stoller, M. A. (1987). The propensity to save among the elderly. *The Gerontoogist, 27*(3), 314–320.

16   Action for Independent Maturity. (1983). *AIMs guide to estate planning.* Washington, DC: American Association of Retired Persons.

Chapter Ten

Retirement Preparation Programs

This chapter reviews the interest of some employers in providing part-time employment opportunities for their employees, thus easing the transition into retirement. The need for preretirement programs is emphasized. Case studies of some existing programs are given, and future directions are proposed, for the information of both older persons who are planning to retire or have already retired and employers considering the development of preretirement programs for their employees. The implications for counselors of preretirement programs are indicated and some group activities are listed to encourage attention to the development of such programs.

Formalized planning for retirement seems to be a fairly recent activity and one in which a relatively small number of persons participate. This activity has been labeled in the past by various titles: preretirement education, preretirement counseling, and retirement planning, to name a few. The term *retirement preparation* seems to be more inclusive and, hence, is used in this chapter.

An increasing social consciousness in the 1960s and growing concern for older persons in American society had the effect of focusing attention on several issues, including the conditions and circumstances of their retirement from the labor force. In the 1970s, federal legislation included such topics as retirement age and mandatory retirement (Age Discrimination in Employment Act Amendments, 1978), and pension policies (Employee Retirement Income Security Act of 1974). Actual and projected increases in the numbers of older persons, along with the expanding life span, alerted both federal and state agencies to the importance of the quality of life after retirement.

Other factors have contributed to a greater interest in retirement preparation: the activities of the labor unions in supporting favorable living conditions for workers in retirement and the influence of the national organizations of retired persons. For example, an Industry Consortium Development Program was organized in 1978 by the National Council on the Aging (1). Nine major corporations participated with four labor unions to discuss and implement retirement planning for their organizations. The American Association for Retired Persons (AARP) developed in 1978 a retirement preparation program titled Action for Independent Maturity (AIM).

INNOVATIVE APPROACHES TO CONTINUED EMPLOYMENT AND RETIREMENT

More recently, the emphasis of AARP has been on various types of full- and part-time jobs that can result in delaying retirement or making the transition to retirement a more gradual process for older workers. In 1986, AARP published a booklet entitled "Managing a Changing Work Force" that described major alternatives.

The Institute of Gerontology at the University of Michigan organized a computerized data collection project in the 1980s, supported by funds from the Administration on Aging. Known as the National Older Workers Information Systems (NOWIS), this project focused on innovative practices by U. S. companies in providing employment opportunities for older workers (defined as those over 50 years of age). A total of 369 such practices were assembled from 180 companies (2). Although these practices are not widely used, they do provide examples of ways in which companies can address the twin issues of the continued employment and retirement of older workers. It should be noted that these practices are of mutual benefit to the company and to the older employee. The following are the categories of practices included in NOWIS.

Part- and Full-Time Employment

Employing older workers part time represents more than one-third of the special practices described in NOWIS. Employment pools have been established to enable personnel to meet temporary labor needs. Such pools may consist of former employees who want only part-time work. The special advantage of this arrangement is that the company's retirees require little start-up time.

Some companies hire back retirees on a project basis, gaining the use of particular talents. To avoid possible adverse effects of rehiring on pension benefits, companies may develop contractual relationships with retirees. Also, changes may be made in the pension structure. This situation is no problem when the employment pools consist only of older workers from other companies.

Older workers may be employed on a full-time basis if their particular skills are in short supply. They may be hired because they have certain desirable qualities usually associated with age. For example, they are less likely to be transient residents, and they tend to develop better relationships with older customers.

Older workers are described as a valuable resources for companies in a publication by the National Alliance of Business (3). Among the management objectives listed for employing older workers is the stabilization of the younger workforce. The logic is that older workers are often role models for younger workers, illustrating qualities of a solid work ethic, loyalty, and stability.

This same publication also indicates that employers frequently are taking active roles to help older workers in their transition to retirement. In addition to assisting with financial planning, some companies are encouraging their older workers to consider second careers, various employment options, and volunteer community service roles.

Transitions to Retirement

A number of companies have developed various alternatives to the retirement event. One is to offer a reduction in the number of hours worked per day or weeks per month for one or more years prior to retirement. Polaroid Corporation offers "Rehearsal Retirement," in which workers may take as long as 6 months of unpaid vacation to test the lifestyle before applying for retirement (4).

A third alternative is "phased retirement," whereby workers have the option to retire, collect their pension, and work part time at an agreed percentage of their preretirement salary. This arrangement is available to employees of Corning Glass Works who are 58 years of age and older, have a record of 20 years of service with the company, and have a type of job in which a 2-day-per-week schedule will handle the workload without the need for hiring a new person (4). This alternative can also provide for the gradual training of the retiree's replacement. A variation of this alternative is "social service" or "personal growth" leaves, through which workers can examine various possibilities for postretirement activities.

Job Redesign

Some companies have redesigned certain of their jobs to meet production changes and the preferences of their employees. Flextime is one example. Here, the product is most important; the scheduling of the time required to create the product is variable. One variation of flextime is performance of the job away from the work site, at home, for example. With the expanded use of computers, this arrangement has become more realistic than ever. Control Data Corporation is an obvious illustration; they have provided computer terminals at the homes of workers.

One further approach to job redesign is job sharing. Under this arrangement, employees are permitted to split a full-time job into two part-time jobs. Some companies have found that delegating this task to employees produces the best results in terms of job performance and worker satisfaction. In the case of the Minnesota Title Financial Corporation, older employees split the jobs of "interoffice messengers" and "foot messengers." (The latter delivers documents within the city.) Two employees divide the time in half, or they work alternate months.

NEED FOR PRERETIREMENT PROGRAMS

Two factors have had a major impact on the need for retirement preparation. The first is that individuals are living longer and, consequently, have more time to live and enjoy living. The second is that retirement from full-time employment is now regarded as a right, and workers are retiring at somewhat earlier ages than in previous years.

There is an emerging third factor: Since the retirement period represents a different lifestyle for many older persons, *earlier* exposure to relevant information regarding retirement appears more and more important. One example is financial planning. Since adequate financial resources are so vital to the retirement years, a lifetime of financial preparation becomes imperative, including a wise allocation of income year by year. A second example is health planning. Health in later years is often a reflection of regular exercise and diet programs in earlier years.

The point is that retirement preparation should really be an integral part of ongoing programs of public and private education. These programs should help to prepare young people not only for entry into the world of work but also into the world of retirement, after full-time work! Education for later life should be understood as a preparation for changes in lifestyles, changes in roles, changes in philosophy of living, and changes in point of view toward others and toward oneself.

Current information about active preretirement programs is not readily available. A 1981 study indicated that about 14% of the 1,000 manufacturing firms listed by *Fortune* magazine returned a questionnaire survey stating that they had preretirement preparation programs, some of which were of limited scope (5).

At the present time, AARP conducts 3-day meetings for representatives of industrial or business organizations, educational institutions, chambers of commerce, and banks planning to develop preretirement programs. These meetings are well attended, suggesting a continuing interest. However, it would appear that preretirement programs are sustained principally by employers who maintain a large work force among the 1,000 listed by *Fortune* Magazine (4). Employees of smaller organizations are less likely to have exposure to such programs.

The greater numbers of group preretirement programs can be described as illustrating one of three models: planning, counseling, or adult education (6). Most often used has been the planning model, which assumes that retirement is an economic event that will result in financial restrictions, without reference to psychological factors. On the other hand, the counseling model focuses on social and psychological issues in retirement. It is assumed that personal problems will develop, and therefore positive attitudes toward retirement are encouraged. The adult education model assumes that retirement is a life stage in which fundamental changes will occur in retirees' life patterns. One major goal of this model is to build self-esteem. Another is to encourage further education in order to build a new career and find a new job.

Giordano and Herwig-Giordano (6) described a new possibility, which they called the human potential model. This model draws on the counseling and adult education models, but emphasizes retirement as a time of self-renewal in which the retiree is seen as a mature adult, a total person. This person has physical, social, mental, and spiritual elements and needs, and each must be addressed in a preretirement program that is intended to emphasize development of positive attitudes and new lifestyles. This model requires special attention to individual involvement in the group process as well as skilled leaders who can facilitate the process.

CASE STUDIES

Some case studies of various preretirement programs may be helpful for counselors working with preretirees or for persons considering development of such programs. Those described below are intended to illustrate particular approaches to employee retirement. They are not necessarily evaluated as superior to others that have not been included.

Kimberly-Clark Corporation

The Kimberly-Clark Corporation participated in the Industry Consortium Development Program initiated in 1977 by the National Council on the Aging. It has maintained an active interest in preretirement planning for its employees since that time. During the past 4 years the program has not been changed in any major way. Training materials have been updated and different speakers have been invited from time to time.

The major procedural change in this program has been that employees, with their spouses, are invited to participate when they are 50 years of age or older. In earlier years, the minimum age was 55. The lecture method is used for the presentation of information; group discussion is encouraged. Retired Kimberly-Clark employees are frequently asked to be discussion leaders.

Various topics are presented during 4 consecutive weeks at one evening meeting per week. These meetings are 2–3 hr long.

The general objective is to encourage employees to begin planning for their retirement years and to recognize that retirement is a very personal experience. The point is made that this is perhaps the only time in life when individuals can do their own planning, set their own priorities, and decide on the directions they will take. Major topics covered are

1 Personal health and attitudes toward the aging process;
2 Financial planning, including company benefits at retirement (the company's pension plan is discussed in detail);
3 Social Security, Medicare, and Kimberly-Clark medical insurances;
4 Estate planning, legal affairs, wills, and trusts;
5 Retirement living, insights from company retirees (this topic area may include use of leisure time, housing and housing location, education, and work opportunities).

Selected handout materials are part of each lecture session.

Florida Power Corporation

The Florida Power Corporation's preretirement program is called "Future Focus." It has been well received by employees and is recommended by administrative staff. Said one administrator, "I encourage all corporations or institutions to conduct pre-retirement programs."

This program consists of three full-day workshops and is available to employees and their spouses. Its primary purpose is to help employees learn how to meet the life changes associated with retirement. More specifically, its objectives are to ease the retirement transition, eliminate emotional stress, clarify benefit plans, emphasize financial stability through planning, and promote employee morale overall.

Topics are organized into three major categories. The first is general orientation to the preretirement program, with emphasis on the major sources of retirement income: Social Security and how to apply and the corporation's pension plan and how it operates.

The second category is financial planning, with detailed information and discussion about life insurance; medical insurance; the corporation's stock option plan; various savings plans, including IRAs; making wills and estate planning; preparation of federal income tax forms; and maximizing pension income through investment alternatives.

The third category, postretirement planning, covers a variety of topics including health maintenance; further educational opportunities; physical fitness and the aging process; volunteer programs, such as the Senior Mentors program, which enables retirees to assist high school students with their work; and retiree organizations such as the AARP. Finally, all retirement documents are reviewed and explained in detail.

Polaroid Corporation

Polaroid has a comprehensive program designed to aid its employees in their transition from full-time work to full-time retirement. This program has two major features. The first is a planned reduction in work schedules, which enables employees to try out the experience of working less than full time. "Rehearsal Retirement" is a leave of absence without pay for 3 months, on the average. At the end of that time, employees may elect to retire or to return to work at their same job, with their seniority dates adjusted and all benefits resumed.

"Tapering Off" work schedules mean that employees may gradually reduce the number of hours worked each day, number of days worked each week, or the number of weeks worked each month. Individuals are paid for the hours actually worked. Health insurance coverage is maintained in full. The essential elements of these work schedules are flexibility, the prior approval of the employee's supervisor, and departmental needs.

Polaroid's experience with the opportunities given employees to reduce their work schedules has been positive and generally successful. Approximately 50% who have tried retirement on a trial basis have returned to work full time. Others who have retired are interested in taking part-time jobs, even though the pay is less and the status is lower. Apparently, many workers must leave their jobs completely before they can identify the satisfactions they received from working.

The second major feature of Polaroid's program is a number of retirement counseling opportunities. The corporation sponsors a "Life-Planning" seminar series. These seminars are held twice a year in the evening and are available to older employees and their spouses. Each of seven group seminars covers a separate topic: personal financial planning; health and well-being; Social Security in retirement; the retiree's hidden skills; clues to future pursuits; legal planning; living arrangements; and Polaroid retirement plans.

Additional counseling opportunities are provided primarily on an individual basis. One is called the "Window Shopping" conference and is designed to review the financial implications of retirement at different ages. Another is the preretirement conference during which a variety of topics are discussed including attitudes toward retirement, use of leisure time, possible difficulties in the transition, activities in retirement, information regarding retirement benefits, retirement budgets, and providing protection for survivors. "Age 52 Seminars" are scheduled for 4 hr and concentrate on Polaroid's retirement benefits and Social Security.

When the retirement program was started, it was limited to employees age 55 and over and their spouses. This age limit was later reduced to 52.

Kollmorgen Corporation (Electro-Optical Division)

The Electro-Optical Division of the Kollmorgen Corporation established a series of preretirement planning seminars in recent years on the basis of two assumptions: (a) Planning for retirement has become increasingly complex so that it should be started well before employees intend to retire, and (b) management can assist by providing employees with information important to their preretirement planning. This series was initiated after management received positive feedback from employees.

The seminars are scheduled for 2 hr each, once a week, for 8 consecutive weeks. They are held in the evenings, with the exception of the introductory seminar, which is held in the afternoon. Since spouses are encouraged to attend, the evening hours appear preferable. Refreshments are served and the atmosphere is informal. Speakers are division employees or outside specialists in particular fields. Attendance at these seminars is entirely voluntary. However, since each seminar is part of a carefully integrated program, participants are expected to attend all eight seminars.

The topics of the seminars are

1 Preretirement planning—why it is critical to life planning for the retirement years;
2 Social Security and health insurance;
3 Kollmorgen Corporation retirement;
4 Investments, trusts, estates, and wills—how the retiree can arrange assets as well as family affairs to his or her greatest advantage;
5 Real estate and housing—their significance in determining the quality of living and lifestyle;
6 Living better, longer, and more productively—suggestions concerning a variety of health and social issues;
7 Employment in retirement, leisure time, and life styles—A variety of alternatives to enable continued productivity through employment, continuing education, and recreation;
8 Looking back on several years of retirement—two or three married couples share their experiences in retirement.

Participants are asked to complete a questionnaire evaluating each seminar in terms of the speakers, the content, and the overall value. Each speaker brings handouts relevant to the discussion topic. One handout is titled "A Checklist of Things to Do Before Retirement." This handout includes five sections on income, health, activities, family and friends, and a place to live. Each section has 5 or 10 action statements indicating a step taken toward retirement relating to the section topic. Employees are asked to review the statements periodically, marking "yes" by those action statements that have been completed. In this way they can evaluate their progress in planning for their own retirement.

Atlantic Richfield Company

Atlantic Richfield has committed itself to a formal continuing preretirement planning program for employees in all operating units. This commitment is based on surveys that indicated that most employees over 50 years of age wanted such a program. The decision was made to use a preretirement program developed by the National Council on the Aging.

Participation in this program is voluntary. It consists of 23 1/2 hr of instruction and focuses on eight retirement issues and what employees and their spouses can do about them. Each issue is considered as a major part of the program. These issues are

1 Lifestyle planning—Self-assessment tools plus group discussion are used to help individuals plan their own futures.

2 Financial planning—Participants develop a personal retirement financial plan.

3 Being healthy—Preventive physical and mental health are stressed through presentations and discussions.

4 Interpersonal relations—Through group discussions and exercises, participants understand how relationships are affected by retirement and how they can lead to happiness in retirement.

5 Community services—Topics include what services are available in the community and how they can help meet participants' needs.

6 Living arrangements—Participants discuss alternative living communities and types of housing for retirement.

7 Leisure time—Various options are discussed and the satisfactions each provides.

8 New careers in retirement—Group discussion is focused on participants' skills and interests, and each individual is encouraged to prepare a personal new career plan.

As noted, group discussion and individual involvement are emphasized, along with special exercises, simulation, case studies, role-playing, and workbooks. At the end of 10 weeks, each participant will have written his or her own preretirement plan. The broad objective is planning and the understanding that retirement changes an individual's life in many ways.

University of Florida

The University of Florida's preretirement planning program is open to all employees; especially encouraged to attend are those who are 55 years of age or older and who have been employed for at least 10 years. It is sponsored by the Division of Human Resources and is scheduled once a week for 3 consecutive weeks during afternoons for 2–3 hr each afternoon during the fall of each year. Refreshments are served each afternoon.

The content emphasis is on financial planning and retirement benefits. The topics covered are

1   University benefits,
2   State retirement benefits and procedures,
3   Social Security benefits,
4   Financial planning for retirement,
5   Estate planning,
6   Retirement: pain or pleasure?,
7   Recreation and fitness.

Programs in Transition

One notable example of the shift by some organizations away from retirement programs is provided by the Bankers Life and Casualty Company, located in Chicago. As of 1983 this company had a series of preretirement seminars titled "Planning for Your Future." Currently, it has no preretirement program.

Executives are reportedly proud that most of their employees reaching age 65 have elected to remain full time at Bankers Life. In fact, company policy now includes hiring qualified people over 65. This company has carried out studies of older employees in the areas of absenteeism, health, and productivity. Its general conclusion is that older workers compare favorably with younger workers in each of these areas.

One specific conclusion is that important contributions to the company are made by the older workers who remain healthy and able to work when they are past 65. This conclusion has led the company to decide that the over-65 life period can be a productive time of life. A company representative has stated that no employees are treated differently because of age. In fact, it was indicated that reaching age 65 is regarded as a "nonevent."

Several companies are in the process of reexamining their preretirement programs, in terms of both content and procedures. Dupont Corporation, for example, offered a day-long session several years ago for the purpose of providing employees with a long-range retirement planning opportunity. That program was discontinued and a new program is being developed that will concentrate on financial planning.

Xerox Corporation has gone from a corporationwide preretirement program to one that is decentralized on a departmental basis. American Express is giving some attention to a preretirement program that has financial planning as its emphasis.

More companies are developing retirement transition programs. Varian Associates in California provides for a reduced work week and proportionately reduced salary for employees planning retirement within about 2 years. Corning Glass Works has a phased retirement program titled "40-Percent Work Option" for salaried professionals. Mutual of New York offers to salaried office workers 1 day off per week at full pay for the 52 weeks before retirement. Wells Fargo and Company in California permits employees of any age to take "social service leave" or "personal growth leave." The amount of time given for these leaves from work depends on the number of years the worker has been employed by the company. Workers applying for these leaves from their jobs must indicate in advance what study or activity they plan to pursue. They must agree to return to the company after their leave and submit a written report detailing the values of the leave for them.

THE FUTURE OF PRERETIREMENT PROGRAMS

In the future, preretirement programs will differ from those presently being used in both timing and content. Some forecasts suggest that in terms of timing, future programs will be scheduled at about the midpoint of the work career so that individuals will have a reasonable opportunity to plan for their retirement and to make the personal adjustments necessary to prepare for that important period in their lives. Also, follow-up programs will be planned for 1 or 2 years before actual retirement.

It is hoped that future planners of preretirement programs will have gained a more positive view of retirement and more specific ideas about retirees' roles in retirement and their needs for preparation to live actively and fully in a world of change. The future will indeed be different from the present (7). Indications are that retirees will live 20–30 years or more after leaving full-time work. They will enjoy better health because of continued participation in regular physical exercise and in the activities of their communities.

They will need to assume more responsibility for their financial security, supplementing their pensions, including Social Security, as necessary. They should be prepared to build a personal budget, handle the investment of personal funds, and seek continued employment, at least part time. If they are part of a four-generation family, they may have responsibility for both younger and older family members as well as for themselves.

Such changing conditions, and others that will undoubtedly occur, will require changes in the content of preretirement programs. At present too many program planners assume that retirees are to be prepared for a condition of dependency. For example, financial planning tends to emphasize the ways in which companies and governments are going to take care of retirees through pensions. More and more, retirees will need to find more ways to take care of themselves. The emphasis on wills and estate planning may be premature or out of place for retirees who will live for 20–30 more years. Future preretirement programs should be based on the assumption that retirees are to be prepared to maintain an independent lifestyle and to develop for themselves new initiatives for adapting to change and creating meaningful ways of living. Topics to be considered for future programs might well include the following:

1 Information regarding a changing U.S. society, the relevant social and economic issues involved, and how these issues might affect retirees.
2 How to develop attitudes of self-reliance and personal responsibility; in the process, reviewing the aging process and changes that will occur therein.
3 Information and training in developing such personal skills as
  (a) managing life transitions,
  (b) setting personal goals,
  (c) making decisions,
  (d) planning second and third work careers,
  (e) managing money.
4 How to develop personal programs for physical and mental health, as well as information about available local resources.
5 Information regarding insurance, especially health insurance.
6 Strengthening of personal relationships with family members, friends, and new acquaintances; building support systems.
7 Information regarding life-planning issues and techniques.

Preretirement programs will be tailored to meet the needs of particular groups of retirees. These programs will also meet the needs of employers by producing continuing employees who are more satisfied with themselves and their relationships and more confident about their future. In the future, preretirement programs will increase in numbers and effectiveness. They will be used by more and more organizations as employers turn to helping employees plan better for their future.

An additional approach in the future to preretirement planning may be for appropriate public and private agencies to use the various news media, especially television, to present pertinent informational programs to the public. Such programs might encourage life planning, both short range and long range by persons of any age, for the basic purpose of building happier lives.

These programs might well be included in the curricula of the various educational systems of this country. For example, colleges and universities now focus on preparing students for their working lives; they might logically extend this preparation to include the quality of life after full-time work. At issue would be the basic goal to be achieved. Would it be to prepare younger and older persons to work more productively? Or would this goal be joined to the more comprehensive one of helping all persons to live happier and more personally rewarding lives over their life spans?

IMPLICATIONS FOR COUNSELORS

The development of preretirement programs in this country reflects the spread of more favorable attitudes about retirement. The emphasis seems to be toward viewing retirement as a more gradual process and increasing opportunities for part-time work.

Some of the larger corporations, but not many, have preretirement programs and others are exploring the possibilities. However, the need is not viewed currently as urgent. Few of the smaller companies with less than 1,000 employees have any preparation programs for employees about to retire.

If it is assumed that retirement preparation is important to older persons, one question to be asked is, How can more workers be exposed to retirement information? And what kinds of information would be most helpful to them? There are several possible answers to the first question. More organizations with a minimum of 200 workers can be encouraged to adopt preretirement programs. Several organizations within the same geographical area can consider joint programs with shared funding. Educational institutions, particularly high schools and community colleges, might develop preretirement programs to be made available to the employees of any local business or governmental organization that would contribute to the funding.

The second question, regarding some evaluation of the various elements of preretirement programs, involves research projects that could be funded by the organizations directly concerned and/or by research foundations, especially those interested in older persons.

By and large, most preretirement programs concentrate on financial planning and helping retirees to understand what financial support they can expect from their pensions or from Social Security. Some additional topics are sometimes added, such as lifestyle planning, use of leisure time, and deciding where to live. The focus appears to be on withdrawal from work.

A new approach to preretirement programming should be considered, one with a forward look that has as its principal purpose preparing retirees for major changes in life and living. Such a program should help retirees build attitudes of independence, self-reliance, and personal responsibility. It should provide training in the refinement of personal skills that would strengthen retirees' capacity for maintaining independent lifestyles for as long as possible. It should encourage positive approaches to the third period of life. It should see this period as one of potential richness, to be enjoyed to the fullest.

GROUP ACTIVITIES

I Give to each member of the group the assignment of developing, in writing, a preretirement program. Only topical headings should be indicated; no detailed materials should be included. Each should specify the nature of the organization for which the employees work and their general needs to be met by the particular program. Procedures for presenting the program should be listed. This assignment might be given for completion at home and brought back within 1 or 2 days.

II Group members should have the opportunity to present verbal reports of their programs, summarizing the major features. Reaction comments and suggestions from other group members should be encouraged.

REFERENCES

1 Fitzpatrick, E. W. (1978). An industry consortium approach to retirement planning—a new program. *Aging and Work, 1*(3), 181–188.
2 Root, L. S. (1985). *Corporate programs for older workers.* In Cox, H. (Ed.), *Aging* (5th ed., pp. 149–153). Gilford, CT: Dushkin.
3 National Alliance of Business. (1985). *New directions for an aging workforce.* Washington, DC: Author.
4 American Association of Retired Persons. (1986). *Managing a changing work force.* Washington, DC: Author.
5 Olson, S. K. (1981). Current status of corporate retirement preparation programs. *Aging and Work, 4*(3), 175–187.
6 Giordano, J. A., & Herwig-Giordano, N. (1982, April). *A classification of preretirement programs: In search of a new model.* Presented at the annual meeting of the Southern Gerontological Society, Atlanta, GA.
7 Loftus, D. F. (1988, February). For older workers and retirement planners. Complex issues, no easy answers. Washington, DC: *AARP Aging Network News,* pp. 4–10.

Chapter Eleven

A New Beginning

In this chapter retirement is redefined as a period of self-discovery and self-renewal. Personal needs are explored and major life transitions reviewed. It is proposed that there are various areas of opportunity to be used by retirees in their enjoyment of living. Advantages in aging are discussed as bases for a new sense of personal freedom, a new lifestyle, and a new beginning for one's life. The implications for counselors are indicated, together with important qualities required for counselors who serve older persons. Group activities are presented as means for clarifying participants' points of view toward the opportunity for enjoying living in retirement and the advantages in aging.

Positive attitudes about the process of aging can be acquired even by those living in contemporary U. S. society. Realizing that aging means growing and that each stage of life is one further step in an exciting growth process can create positive images of aging within individuals about themselves.

Each life stage can be understood as a base for the succeeding life stage; one builds on another toward that ultimate stage that represents the fruition of the individual's life process. Here persons can and do blossom as unique human personalities. The new beginning toward a fuller enjoyment of living comes when individuals see the achievement of personal success and happiness as occurring at the top of the life-stage ladder. Expecting this achievement only half-way or so up this ladder is to cut short the potentials of the life process and to abandon the latter half of life to the bare existence level.

People living in the worlds of today and tomorrow have unique opportunities for personal growth and development. They have greater lengths of time to live, greater resources to use in making the most of their longer lives, and broader visions of their world and the human potential to expand their horizons.

In contrast to this picture of the future is the unfavorable view that some human beings have of themselves. Too many see only their limitations. By narrowly limiting their goals, and failing to see or to develop their potentials, they severely handicap their own growth. A new beginning occurs when individuals look at themselves as their most valuable asset.

When this change truly takes place, every stage of life becomes precious and is to be exploited, hopefully to the satisfaction of the persons most concerned. This point of view makes retirement a life stage to be cultivated and enjoyed, like every other life stage. How should this life stage be really pictured in the minds of individuals?

RETIREMENT REDEFINED

Most definitions describe retirement in terms of withdrawing from full-time work and being taken care of through pensions or government subsidies of some sort. These features are often part of retirement. But retirement means freedom to do and be what individuals have always wanted to do and be, personal satisfactions gained through associations with others, and participation in community life. Retirement, then, truly becomes a time of involvement in living, including part-time work. It is a time for the enjoyment of life. Individuals have the opportunity to discover new interests and talents that have been largely latent all their lives.

Retirement should be a time when individuals discover themselves, perhaps for the first time, and when the real meanings in their lives become clearer to them. In this period of discovery, individuals may learn who they are and what values they really support. Their personal philosophy of life emerges as a guide for living. They become more self-reliant, with a sense of responsibility for themselves. They see new opportunities for service to others and, at the same time, for enrichment of their own lives. The midlife era is a time when most persons devote their efforts to the success of their jobs. In retirement, the emphasis shifts and people can focus on themselves and their own success in living. When individuals spotlight their interests toward themselves and their enjoyment of living through others, they have made a new beginning.

NEEDS TO BE MET

This spotlight on self is likely to illuminate a number of personal needs that individuals should attempt to meet in order to increase the probability of their success and happiness in retirement.

Setting Goals

In Chapter 4 setting goals was described as a vital part of life planning, for individuals of all ages. This need may not be recognized by older persons who have been conditioned by their society to believe that the constructive periods of their lives are essentially over. Overcoming this belief is an important task. One way to do so is to decide on a goal, consider the courses of action to be taken in achieving it, and follow through on one preferred action plan.

For example, establishing a new lifestyle may appear difficult—and it sometimes is. Here is the course of action taken by a physician who retired from his active practice. He took a job with a medical supply company, driving one of the vans that delivered supplies to customers in towns neighboring the one in which he lived. This job enabled him to remain active, to be out of doors, and to have associations with people. He found his new lifestyle enjoyable. Note that this new work was related to his former profession, without many of the responsibilities.

Another example is to decide on a physical activity program to maintain, or regain, good physical health. The first step is a physical examination by a physician to determine one's physical condition. The second step is to plan an exercise program that will strengthen one's physique gradually and uniformly. The third step is to implement this program. This step is particularly important! Even if it calls for walking briskly, a beginning is a walk around the block!

Getting started is often a serious problem. One way is for individuals to begin their mornings by preparing a check-off list of actions that should be taken during the day. One item should be to "exercise for 20 minutes." This list provides a motivation to check off items when completed and to carry over until the next day whatever cannot be completed. Often surprising is this procedure's impact on the individual's reactions of pleasure, sense of accomplishment, and feeling of personal satisfaction. The effect of the exercise activity is usually both physical and mental: Persons feel better in body, mind, and spirit.

Maintaining Physical and Mental Health

People tend to ignore their own state of health, both physical and mental. The extent to which individuals abuse themselves physically, mentally, and emotionally is difficult to understand. This kind of behavior is particularly questionable when more and more people are living longer, 20–30 years or more beyond the time of full-time employment. The issue for these people reaching retirement age is how they want to live, happily or unhappily, effectively or ineffectively, in better or worse states of health. Human beings tend to have within themselves an instinct for survival; they should be helped to have equally strong instincts for satisfaction and enjoyment in living.

Some reduction in physical functioning is as yet an inevitable part of the human condition. Middle-aged and older persons gradually recognize this fact. It is important that they also accept it and adjust their thinking and actions accordingly. Happily, there are generally few appreciable changes in mental functioning associated with aging. As a result mental health becomes increasingly vital to the well-being of older persons.

A starting point for good mental health is to build an appreciation of oneself. This feeling and belief can grow out of experiences in helping other people such as neighbors, ailing members of the church who need visitors, patients in hospitals, or participants in senior center activities. Part-time jobs, hobbies, or work with local government offices can all contribute to individuals' sense of well-being and satisfaction, especially when their desire is to be of service to other persons. Mental health and physical health go together, and one affects the other. For this reason, a regular physical exercise program can enhance a positive self-concept and sense of well-being.

Managing Time

Some older persons approach retirement with the question "What shall I do with all my time?" Often, 6 months or so after retirement, persons say, "I just don't have time to do all the things I want to do" and "I don't see how I ever had time to work before I retired." Managing time is a problem for persons of all ages. One writer on this subject has stated, "To master your time is to master your life and make the most of it" (1, p. 11).

Inability to get things done seems to grow out of four conditions: failing to set priorities, putting things off, trying to get too much done within a given time limit, or attempting to do each task perfectly. As mentioned earlier, a morning checklist of items to be accomplished that day provides the dimensions of the requirements on a person's time. Rating each item in terms of value to the person establishes priorities. Lakein (1) suggested A (high value), B (medium value), and C (low value). When all of their A items are completed, and perhaps some of the B items, retirees can feel good about their day, knowing that the highest value items have been completed. They may also have some "spare" time, when they have put aside the items of low value. The overall result is a feeling of accomplishment and well-being.

Other personal actions seem to contribute to one's ability to manage time. One is organizing papers and possessions. An estimate has been made that 20–30% of one's time is spent in looking for things! Another action is to make schedules that help establish routines for day-to-day living and limit the amount of time spent on any one task. Schedules also enable individuals to include those activities that might otherwise be neglected or overlooked. The net effect is that a degree of balance is gained in life with time allocated for friends, family, exercise, perhaps part-time work, service to others, home chores, and a quiet period for oneself.

Handling Funds

A not uncommon problem for persons approaching retirement is to realize that their experience in handling money matters is limited. In the case of many older men, their experience has involved cashing their pay checks and spending the cash; others may have deposited their checks into a bank checking account, leaving little for savings or investment. In the case of many older women, particularly married women, they may have seldom bothered to write checks, having depended on their spouses to handle the family funds.

Many people, younger and older alike, live up to the limit of their incomes, and some exceed their incomes. The point is that all too many persons do not invest for their futures, putting some money aside to meet future retirement needs. The frequent tendency is for individuals to assume that future financial needs will be met by government and company pensions. However, the closer older persons come to retirement the more likely they are to question whether or not they will have enough money on which to live. Many retirees report that inadequate income is a frequent source of concern.

Handling funds means a number of things. It means investing some cash, with the aim of obtaining the best available rate of interest, as well as shifting funds to sources of higher interest rates. It means care in spending; shopping with an eye for bargains, selecting less costly items, or deciding not to buy when cash is short. It means preparing budgets on a monthly and yearly basis to maintain control over the expenditure of available funds. It means keeping accurate records of checks written, and reconciling bank statements each month.

Retirees can ensure for themselves happier lives by taking time to learn how to handle their money, if they have never had occasion to do so. They can spend sufficient time to maintain careful control over their funds, or they may seek the assistance of a professional financial planner. In any case, the results should be stronger feelings of security and personal satisfaction.

Deciding on Another Career

More older persons are deciding not to retire. According to an American Association of Retired Persons survey, one-third of retirees would rather work. In the case of workers on the job, polls indicate the 51% would prefer to continue working past age 65 (2). There are several reasons: Older persons enjoy better health and are living longer. Living costs continue to increase so that more income is necessary. Many do not have pensions, or, in some instances, their pension programs have been canceled. It is also true that work provides structure and associations that some persons find important to their life satisfaction.

A number of alternatives are available for those looking for second or third careers. They can continue with the same company on a reduced work schedule and sometimes in a different department. Corporations with such programs are described in Chapter 10. Travellers Insurance Company, for example, has an "un-retirement" program for its own retirees as well as those from other companies.

Retirees can turn their hobbies into part-time, paying jobs. One older man had developed the skill of weaving replacements for cane-bottomed chairs as his hobby. When he retired, he created a part-time business of furniture repair.

Companies that provide temporary employee services are recruiting older persons as short-term workers. Kelly Services, for example, has organized a recruitment drive called Encore to attract adults over 55 years of age. Some older persons turn to community colleges for job training in a field they have always regarded as desirable.

Other older persons with little specialized training and limited income seek assistance with such federal agencies as the Senior Community Services Employment Program, Retired Senior Volunteer Program, or Foster Grandparents.

Sizeable numbers of retirees serve as volunteers for a variety of community services, including schools; family-, youth-, and children-oriented services; recreation, health and mental health programs; transportation, such as the home-delivered meals program; housing, such as repairing existing structures; and civic affairs, such as voter registration.

Active participation in civic affairs represents a special opportunity for some retirees who no longer must meet the demands of full-time employment. Some communities across the country find a limited number of citizens who are interested in running for elective positions. Active, informed, and committed retirees represent a source of candidates. Retired business executives who provide advisory services for local business groups illustrate one aspect of the involvement of older persons in community service. Their organization is known as the Service Corps of Retired Executives.

MANAGING LIFE TRANSITIONS

Individuals tend to grow and mature in stages (see Chapter 2). When they accomplish successfully the tasks needed for their development in one stage, they are ready to move on to the next stage. The transition from one stage to another can be a particularly difficult time because it involves meeting new situations, giving up some familiar behaviors and adopting new ones, setting new goals, adjusting values as appropriate to the new stage, and generally accommodating to a variety of changes.

Many persons, younger and older, become accustomed to familiar ways of doing things and resist new and different ways. Overcoming this resistance to change is often a problem, which has several possible causes. One is a lack of confidence in oneself; another is a limited view of oneself and one's future. A third is that personal goals are not clearly defined and have been given no commitment.

Solving this problem of adapting to change seems to involve factors relating to the attitudes of individuals toward aging. If they see change as challenge, if they view aging as growing into more complete persons, if they can release their past life experiences in favor of their future opportunities, then the problem can be largely solved. In the past, the images of aging have been essentially negative. But those images are becoming more positive as health care becomes more available, as more older persons adopt active exercise and nutrition programs, and as they become more involved in the activities of their communities. One definition of an older person is one who looks back rather than forward. That person finds change difficult. The person who looks forward is most likely to resolve problems of change.

Self-confidence is an important personal quality for handling life transitions. Two transition periods can be especially stressful and draw heavily on individuals' confidence. The first is the transition from school to work, which is usually experienced during the late 20s or early 30s. This is a period during which individuals establish their independence from their families, find their place in the world of work, locate partners to join them in building new families, and develop social status in their communities.

The second transition, which is equally demanding, is the change from work to retirement, during the late 60s or 70s. During this period, individuals establish independence from full-time work, create a new lifestyle in the world of retirement, find support partners to give added meaning to their life experiences, and develop a new social status in their communities.

There are two additional transitions. One is the change from physical health to frailty, possibly accompanied by sickness. This change is sometimes gradual, sometimes sudden, and sometimes minimal. Adaptation seems to be better accomplished by those whose interests are focused on others, beyond themselves. For some individuals, considerable willpower is required to direct their attention toward the needs of others, rather than toward themselves. For the majority of older persons, this transition is of minor concern, because they are in reasonable health and generally cope well with physical limitations.

The final transition is from life to death. The fear of dying is one of the reasons that so many people have a negative view of aging and avoid talking about it. However, it is worth noting that some persons lose this fear of dying as they near death and as they think about their lives in global terms, especially events and people who have been significant to them.

For persons facing this transition, it may be helpful, if they have accepted or can accept the stage theory of human development, to see their death as another stage of development, as another part of life. Adopting this point of view can also reduce the fear of dying. Finding ways to overcome this fear is important because it often inhibits and constrains individuals in their abilities to enjoy and get the most out of living.

USING AREAS OF OPPORTUNITY FOR ENJOYING LIVING

The assumption can be made that most older persons have frequent opportunities in their daily environments to enhance the quality of their lives, but such opportunities are often missed because the persons concerned fail to recognize them. Some of the possible areas of opportunity are these:

Finding Ways to Implement Goals. The first step is to have four or five goals very clearly in mind and to give one a top position. During each day, retirees can be looking for one or more ways to implement their top-priority goal as they move around their home or have conversations with others, or in their reading. If nothing seems to fit the top-priority goal, something may apply to one of the other goals. For example, a top-priority goal may be starting an exercise program. In the retiree's conversation with a friend, mention is made of that person's regular walking schedule. The retiree can ask if he or she might join the friend, who often readily agrees. The program is initiated, but first the retiree checks with his or her physician, to make sure that such exercise will be suitable for his or her health status.

As another example, the retiree has the goal of finding a part-time job in a work area in which he or she has no experience but has interest. The local community college advertises on television a new training–placement program in the work area of the retiree's interest. The retiree goes to the college and is accepted into the program.

The importance of having some specific goals is obvious. Without them, retirees would not be sensitive to the opportunity clues that present themselves. In the examples above, the clues came through conversation with a friend and a television announcement.

Keeping Up to Date With Social, Political, and/or Technological Developments. Enjoyment of living tends to be enhanced by the extent to which retirees keep current with the world around them. Sometimes their knowledge base has become obsolescent or even obsolete. This situation results in the legitimate feelings of some retirees that they are out of touch with reality and that their world has passed them by. These feelings can be changed by positive actions such as reading current news magazines; listening to relevant programs on public television stations; joining or forming a discussion group at the local library, church, or senior center; or enrolling in an appropriate course at the local community college. The point is that if retirees do not find existing opportunities they can sometimes create them.

Building a Positive Outlook on Life. Some persons reach the later stage of their lives with an accumulation of negative experiences that have resulted in a negative view of their future. Changing this view from negative to positive can be approached in at least two ways. The retiree can develop a program of active involvement in several community activities that hold a personal interest. In this process, the retiree can establish friendly relationships with other activity participants.

However, it is possible that some retirees may find it difficult to build a positive outlook on life. In this event, they should seek help from a professional counselor, particularly a gerontological counseling specialist. This counselor is likely to review with the retiree those past situations that might have contributed to his or her negative viewpoint. The chances are that some of these situations have been repressed or simply forgotten to the extent that the retiree no longer remembers the circumstances; further, when they are brought back to conscious awareness, they may no longer have any significance.

Developing Personal Support Systems. Retirees' families, especially their adult children, form their strongest support system. However, family relationships cannot be taken for granted but rather should be nurtured. During the later part of parents' lives the roles of family members change; those of the parents shift from dominance in the direction of dependence. Sensitivity of the parents to the changing nature of their roles in relation to those of their adult children will do much to maintain the quality and strength of the family support system.

When this family system no longer exists for retirees, other support systems must be developed. One possibility is community organizations, including the individuals' church or synagogue. Another is building a close association among a group of friends, with the group giving steady support to each of its members. For example, a number of retired ministers and their families formed such a group within one city. They visited with each other regularly, took turns entertaining the group in their homes for special occasions such as Thanksgiving and Christmas, and provided assistance for members who became sick or needed help with special problems.

The value of support groups to retirees' self-concepts and to their needs for reassurance and encouragement is great. It should also be noted that developing a support group takes initiative and positive action on the part of retirees, as well as self-understanding and a willingness to consider and support in fair measure the preferences of others in the relationship.

Fostering a Positive View of Aging. All of the above-described areas of opportunity for enjoying one's retirement more will contribute to a positive view of aging, particularly one's own aging. In addition, retirees need to survey quite frankly their own attitudes and feelings about growing older. The possibilities are that they are largely negative because of societal indoctrinations. Older persons in this situation have several courses of action they can follow. First, they can ask themselves, "What is my negative view of aging doing to me and my enjoyment of living?" If the answer is "I'm not enjoying myself," efforts should be made to shift this negative view in positive directions.

In addition, retirees might focus on getting acquainted with some other older persons, preferably about their own age, and mentally listing favorable qualities of those persons and observing their approach to life. Further, it could be useful to join an activity that has as its principal objective providing assistance to older persons, for example, the Friendly Visitors or Telephone Reassurance programs. These programs usually are conducted through senior centers. Helping other older persons often has the result of increasing one's understanding and appreciation of them as human beings.

As another course of action aimed at building a positive view of aging, retirees might enroll in a course or seminar on the subject of the aging process. Gaining information about aging can suggest to them what they might anticipate for themselves, removing in some measure fear of the unknown. Also retirees could benefit from participation in a discussion of aging in small groups with other retirees. A further action might be for retirees to consider and write down on paper in outline form what they see as advantages to be gained from living in the later stage of their life span.

ADVANTAGES IN AGING

One writer suggests that people tend to have three or four peaks of achievement in their lives, occurring at about ages 30, 50, and 70 (3). Associated with them are feelings of great energy and the renewal of life power. Maslow has reported that after a serious illness in his 60s, the events of everyday living were much more meaningful (4). One of the advantages to be found in aging, then, is discovering and enjoying oneself as well as the physical and social environment within which one lives. The opportunity at this time of life is being oneself and enriching one's own life.

A second advantage is rediscovering and enjoying the other people in one's life, for example, renewing and strengthening relationships with one's spouse. Over the years, couples can grow apart, especially when both are employed. When one or both retire and spend more time together, they may need to become reacquainted. The chances are that both have changed since the early days of their marriage and the process of sharing themselves anew with each other can be stimulating and enjoyable. For those retirees who do not have a spouse, establishing new friendships can be most rewarding.

A third advantage is that retirees are freed in sizable measure from the demands of a daily work schedule set by someone else. Much of the time and energy spent in meeting these demands can be redirected to individual's personal preferences and projects. As a result, retirees can arrange their own schedule, set their own priorities, and enjoy flexibility in using their time and energy. But this kind of freedom in retirement does not mean doing nothing. It means having opportunities to pursue special interests, to engage in activities that enrich one's life and to live more fully. It means the adoption of more personal goals and the expenditure of more personal energy in order to benefit from this new freedom.

A fourth advantage in aging is the additional opportunities to escape the limits of time and space, to dream about living more fully, and to discover more creative ways to achieve one's potential. But dreams must be translated into action, and this includes examining one's value system and deciding whether or not it is appropriate to the one's present lifestyle. This process can be difficult, but reviewing one's values can be a wonderful opportunity to better understand oneself.

Perhaps the greatest advantage in aging is realizing that one's new freedom in retirement has been well earned. As retirees review their past lives and plan for their present and future lives, they can find much satisfaction in both their past accomplishments and present opportunities for a new changed lifestyle.

This process of life review can arouse negative feelings about certain past events. However, this process can become positive when retirees assess the causes for their negative feelings and find that, by and large, these causes are no longer important, and the negative feelings can be put to rest (5). The resulting sense of freedom can led to a new attitude toward living, with older persons seeing their world in new terms. Living then takes on new meanings.

A sixth advantage in aging is learning or relearning to enjoy pleasure for its own sake. According to Dangott and Kalish, "Pleasure is a celebration of the self and a style of relating to others" (6, p. 140). The difficulty is that many persons have lived with the belief that feeling good for the pleasure of feeling good is basically wrong; the important value has been work, and the important activities in life have been those that are economically productive. Yet, cheerfulness, laughter, happiness, and pleasure in living are important features of growing older successfully.

Bloomfield and Kory have written about the importance of experiencing pleasure and the value of inner joy as bases for successful living for all persons of any age. For them, inner joy is an internal state of being, an emotional foundation for one's energy, self-confidence, and choice of the positive over the negative (7). Fromme sees laughter as contributing to one's quality of life (8).

Discovering these and other advantages in aging is very much an individual matter. People have quite different views about personal enjoyment and how they would define enjoying life and living. A common problem is that some people need help in understanding what enjoyment is and how to enjoy themselves outside of a full-time work setting. These are people who seem to be unable to adjust to using nonwork time, who feel that only working at a paying job during a work week can justify the time they spend enjoying leisure activities. Such people may require the assistance of a professional counselor.

IMPLICATIONS FOR COUNSELORS

Major purposes of this book have been to encourage individuals in the middle years of their lives to learn more about the process of growing older and to present information that might prove useful to them. An additional purpose has been to help readers understand the importance of looking for and taking advantage of the significant opportunities to be found in growing older. After individuals recognize and overcome the frequently held myths about aging, they can be better prepared to enjoy its realities. A most important point is that each phase or stage of a person's life has many advantages and using them for one's benefit and happier living is infinitely to be desired.

Counselors usually enjoy working with older persons, either retired or not yet retired, because of the range of their experiences and the comparatively broad time span they encompass. However, certain qualities and abilities are required of those who serve as counselors for older people.

First, counselors need to look at their own views of aging and retirement. Are these views positive or negative? Do they reflect American society's commonly held misconceptions about aging and retirement?

Second, on the assumption that these views are basically negative, counselors will require some advance preparation in order to be most effective with older clients. Such preparation would include seminars on the process of aging and the life changes that typically occur. Additional preparation should consider gathering information relevant to older persons regarding their maintaining physical and mental health, developing effective relationships with others, using time effectively, handling finances, and creating new lifestyles.

Third, counselors should be especially trained to assist older clients in identifying their major needs, prioritizing them, and reviewing appropriate courses of action to take. Fourth, counselors should be alert to the opportunities their clients might expect to find in retirement and explore with them the advantages in growing older.

Fifth, counselors should be prepared to discuss with clients their philosophy of life, especially their feelings about the enjoyment of living for its own sake. To see the life span as a totality with each stage contributing to the meaning of the whole can be an exciting objective of counselors for their older clients. This overall view can also be used to assist older clients through the transition periods between life stages.

GROUP ACTIVITIES

Review with the group the various possible areas of opportunity that older persons might look for to assist them in enjoying retirement living. After this review ask group members where they might look for similar opportunities in their own lives.

Ask group members to form two subgroups, with one discussing the advantage of aging and the other the disadvantages of aging. Request individual members to react to the reports of the two groups, including which report they would want to incorporate into their own lives, and why.

REFERENCES

1 Lakein, A. (1973). *How to get control of your time and your life.* Bergenfield, NJ: New American Library.
2 American Association of Retired Persons. (1986). *Managing a changing work force.* Washington, DC: Author.
3 Gresham, P. E. (1980). *With wings as eagles.* Winter Park, FL: Anna G.
4 Puner, M. (1979). *Vital maturity: Living longer and better.* New York: Universe Books.
5 Butler, R. N. (1975). *Why survive: Being old in America.* New York: Harper and Row.
6 Dangott, L. R., & Kalish, R. A. (1979). *A time to enjoy the pleasures of aging.* Englewood Cliffs, NJ: Prentice-Hall.
7 Bloomfield, H. H., & Kory, R. B. (1980). *Inner joy.* New York: Playboy Paperbacks.
8 Fromme, A. (1984). *Life after work.* Washington, DC: American Association of Retired Persons.

Index